Walking in the Footsteps of the Buddha:
The Path to Freedom

by
Ven. Khenchen Palden Sherab Rinpoche
and
Ven. Khenpo Tsewang Dongyal Rinpoche

Walking in the Footsteps of the Buddha: The Path to Freedom

by
Ven. Khenchen Palden Sherab Rinpoche
and
Ven. Khenpo Tsewang Dongyal Rinpoche

Edited by the Samye Translation Group
Amanda Lewis

Walking in the Footsteps of the Buddha:
The Path to Freedom

Copyright © 2019   Khenpo Tsewang Dongyal Rinpoche

Published by Dharma Samudra.

Padma Samye Ling
618 Buddha Highway
Sidney Center, NY 13839
(607) 865-8068
padmasambhava.org

ISBN-13: 978-1-7335411-3-8

DEDICATION

Dedicated in the honor and memory of His Holiness Dudjom Rinpoche,
Venerable Khenchen Palden Sherab Rinpoche, Lama Chimed Namgyal,
and all the lineage holders of these secret teachings, as well as all the devoted
practitioners of the past, present, and future.

CONTENTS

༄༅། །སྐྱབས་འགྲོ་དང་སེམས་བསྐྱེད།

REFUGE AND BODHICHITTA

༄༅། །སངས་རྒྱས་ཆོས་དང་ཚོགས་ཀྱི་མཆོག་རྣམས་ལ ། །

SANG JE CHÖ DANG TSOG CHI CHOG NAM LA

To the excellent Buddha, Dharma and Sangha

བྱང་ཆུབ་བར་དུ་བདག་ནི་སྐྱབས་སུ་མཆི། །

JANG CHUB BAR DU DAG NI CHAB SU CHI

I go for refuge until the attainment of enlightenment.

བདག་གིས་སྦྱིན་སོགས་བགྱིས་པའི་བསོད་ནམས་ཀྱིས། །

DAG GI JIN SOG JI PE SÖ NAM CHI

By the merits of generosity and other paramitas by me

འགྲོ་ལ་ཕན་ཕྱིར་སངས་རྒྱས་འགྲུབ་པར་ཤོག །

DRO LA PEN CHIR SANG JE DRUB PAR SHOG

May I attain buddhahood for the sake of sentient beings.

Repeat three times

༄༅། །ཚད་མེད་བཞི།

FOUR BOUNDLESS

༄༅། །སེམས་ཅན་ཐམས་ཅད་བདེ་བ་དང་བདེ་བའི་རྒྱུ་དང་ལྡན་པར་གྱུར་ཅིག །

**SEM CHEN TAM CHE DE WA DANG DE WE JU DANG
DEN PAR JUR CHIG**

May all beings have happiness and the cause of happiness.

སྡུག་བསྔལ་དང་སྡུག་བསྔལ་གྱི་རྒྱུ་དང་བྲལ་བར་གྱུར་ཅིག །

**DUG NGAL DANG DUG NGAL JI JU DANG DRAL WAR
JUR CHIG**

May they be free from suffering and the cause of suffering.

སྡུག་བསྔལ་མེད་པའི་བདེ་བ་དམ་པ་དང་མི་འབྲལ་བར་གྱུར་ཅིག །

**DUG NGAL ME PE DE WA DAM PA DANG MI DRAL
WAR JUR CHIG**

May they never be dissociated from the supreme happiness
which is without suffering.

ཉེ་རིང་ཆགས་སྡང་གཉིས་དང་བྲལ་བའི་བཏང་སྙོམས་ཚད་མེད་པ་ལ་གནས་པར་
གྱུར་ཅིག །

**NYE RING CHAG DANG NYI DANG DRAL WE TANG
NYOM TSE ME PA LA NE PAR JUR CHIG**

May they remain in boundless equanimity, free from both
attachment to close ones and rejection of others.

Repeat three times

Buddha Shakyamuni

INTRODUCTION

FINDING EVERLASTING JOY, PEACE, AND HAPPINESS

All the enlightened beings and great wisdom teachers, including Buddha Shakyamuni, Guru Padmasambhava, and the lineage masters of Tibetan Buddhism, have said the same thing: in order to truly make our lives more meaningful, there's nothing to turn to other than love, compassion, joy, appreciation, and devotion. This isn't religious dogma or something someone said that we should blindly follow and believe. It's simply true.

With this understanding, as our great teacher Khenchen Palden Sherab Rinpoche and all the great lineage masters often said, every day and in every practice session, we should continually restrengthen our beautiful motivation of joy, devotion, and *bodhichitta*. That's our practice: it's what we would like to actualize, and that's why we're following the Buddha's teachings. Every teaching the Buddha gave is about love, compassion, wisdom, respect, appreciation, and on being more humble, simple, and practical. That's what all the teachings are about. This is our base, our foundation, and our home.

Over the years, I've repeated what these great masters have said so many times, again and again. I'm not saying this to sound like a broken record—I truly feel that this is what's most important. We're following in the footsteps of the great peacemakers and masters who remove the suffering and difficulties of all sentient beings and bring them everlasting joy, peace, and happiness. How wonderful, how beautiful, and how truly glorious it is!

If we get to the heart of the matter, there really aren't many things in this world that are more important than what we're talking about now. We aren't talking about someone else's qualities—this is our very own treasure and goodness! This is what we'd like to explore, glorify, and this is what we practice. So bring that up to the surface! Don't let it get lost in the midst of duality and unhealthy habitual patterns. Bring it up from the bottom to the top and let it shine! Let it shine out in every direction—at the top, in the middle, on the bottom, and deep down. This is so important and so special.

What I'm talking about is something you can apply in every meditation practice—and not just in every meditation session, but as you begin each day, and with every breath you take. We shouldn't only apply this occasionally, or once in a blue moon—this is the practice itself. As all the great masters have said, you have to start with the foundation, with the very ground where you're standing. There's no way we can hover in the sky all the time. Maybe once in a while we can jump off a cliff with a glider, and if we're lucky, we can fly around for fifteen or thirty minutes, but otherwise, we have to stand on the ground. From there we can deepen and grow tall and strong, and from there we can fly like birds, or *garudas* that don't depend on any other means of support. In order to do this, we need the "four renunciation thoughts."

Simply put, the four renunciation thoughts are contemplations on: (1) our precious opportunity, (2) impermanence, (3) cause and effect, and (4) how life is filled with difficulties.

The four renunciation thoughts also aren't something we just think about once in a while. We should reflect on them during every practice session. The great master Khenpo Ngakchung and many others have said that if we don't contemplate the four renunciation thoughts at the beginning of our session, our practice won't be smooth because it will just hover on the surface our brain and not absorb into our heart. We'd like to make our entire practice meaningful—from the time we start until we conclude—so that it completely absorbs into our heart. This makes beautiful, perfect, quality practice that isn't just a historical record of how long we practiced.

For example, what does it actually mean to go on retreat? Retreat means that we're absorbing the teachings into our hearts. The teachings shouldn't just go in one ear and out the other as an emergency exit. That isn't retreat and it isn't practice. During retreat, we're going to absorb the teachings into the heart so we perfectly blend ourselves with the Dharma; so that we become the teaching. That's what retreat is.

In order to do this, the four renunciations are so important. The essence of renunciation is joy, appreciation, joyful effort, and being thoughtful to make every activity useful and beneficial. What do I mean by every activity? There are three primary activities: body activities, speech activities, and mind activities. We ourselves have to be thoughtful about these activities—we can't expect that someone else is going to be thoughtful for us. We're not going to use any scapegoat, or blame another person or object. When it comes to our own heart and our own practice, we're going to take full responsibility for ourselves. So we need to be thoughtful with the activities of our body, with what we say, and with our mental activities.

Thoughts are the starting point of all our verbal and physical activities. Every movement we make and everything we say—it's all reflected and ignited from our unseen emptiness mind. Everything begins with the mind. Therefore, we need to be very thoughtful.

And have courage! In *samsara* there are so many difficulties and troubles—we all know this. But as the Buddha said, it's a learning opportunity, it's exercise, and it's a playground! Therefore, be courageous and strong, without being so sensitive and perishable, easily getting knocked over like a blade of grass or a feather. Be strong. That is the essence of the four renunciations thoughts.

With this understanding, we also need to reflect on the causes and effects of samsara. Samsara has causes and it has effects. To avoid the effects and move away from them, we follow a path. The path that was taught in the Buddha's first teaching is known as the *Noble Eightfold Path*. The Eightfold Path is the starting point of our journey so that we can begin to apply the teachings in our lives in a more tangible way. Again, following in the footsteps of the great masters, all eight of those paths can be summarized into the *Three Trainings*. We'll go into these in more detail later, but the three extraordinary personal trainings are: (1) morality, (2) concentration, and (3) wisdom.

Morality is more related with our physical and verbal outreaching activities that other people can see and feel. Being moral or ethical is both good for you as an individual and good for others. It also means making a good example of yourself in a way that inspires yourself and others.

How important is morality in the Buddha's teachings? To give an example, one of the Buddha's first five students was known as Tathul in Tibetan. The way Tathul acted, spoke, and the way he moved was so gentle, so beautiful and peaceful. The teachings always say that the great *arhat* masters—those stainless realization beings—were like a chain of golden mountains surrounding a single, larger golden mountain, which was the Buddha himself. Among all the students of the Buddha—among all the glowing golden mountains of arhats— Tathul behaved the best. Buddha acknowledged and announced this by saying, "Tathul's conduct is the best among all the arhats."

In the Padma Samye Ling temple we have statues of Shariputra and Maudgalyaputra on the right and left sides of the Buddha. They were also great disciples of Buddha Shakyamuni. Shariputra first became a disciple of Buddha Shakyamuni because he was so inspired by Tathul's conduct. The way Tathul dressed and moved, the way he spoke and gazed—it was so uplifting. Near the bamboo groves of Rajagriha of central northern India, Shariputra was far away when he first saw Tathul. Shariputra thought, "That person must be someone very special. He must have got the nectar. He looks like a completely nourished person. I must make contact with him to find out where he got such a nourishing, nectar-like quality."

Tathul's gestures, movements, and conduct were so appealing, uplifting, calming, and beautiful to Shariputra that he immediately went up to him and asked, "Who are you? Who is your teacher? And what has your teacher taught you?" Tathul replied, "I am Tathul and I am a disciple of the great sage known as Buddha Shakyamuni." The moment Shariputra heard the name "Buddha," something completely changed inside of him. It was like something electric went through his veins and completely woke something up. Then Shariputra asked, "What was his teaching? What did he give you?" Then Tathul said, "All things proceed from a cause. The tathagatha has explained their cause. This is the doctrine of the great ascetic." This is just a rough English translation of what we often chant in Sanskrit:

OM YE DHARMA HETU PRABAWA HETUNTESHAN
TATHAGATO HAYAWADAT TESHANCHA YO NIRODHA
EWAM WADI MAHA SHRAMA NAYE SWAHA

When Tathul repeated that one phrase, Shariputra saw the truth and achieved first *bhumi* realization according to *Theravada*.

Shariputra and Maudgalyaputra were best friends and they promised each other that whoever first got the nectar would immediately share it with the other. So as they promised, when Shariputra got the nectar, he thought "I must share this with Maudgalyaputra," and he ran to Maudgalyaputra. Maudgalyaputra could see Shariputra from very far away—his skin and complexion were glowing so beautifully. Maudgalyaputra immediately said, "You look like you got the nectar." Shariputra replied, "Yes, I got the nectar." Maudgalyaputra asked, "What is the nectar?" Shariputra simply repeated what he heard from Tathul. He said it once, twice, and then during the third time, Maudgalyaputra achieved realization. All of this began with Tathul's beautiful outreaching conduct. Morality is like an individual's ornament.

Again, the Eightfold Noble Path can be summarized into the Three Trainings. The first is morality and after that is concentration. Concentration has more to do with an individual's mind. With concentration, we're not just looking at the outer surface—we begin to look inwardly and become more observant. The third training of wisdom is a support for both morality and concentration. When we practice these three, we're following the path of the Buddha: the path to the cessation of suffering, and the realization of enlightenment, or *nirvana*.

CHAPTER 1

WHAT IS BUDDHISM
REALLY ABOUT?

Ven. Khenpo Rinpoches in Bodhgaya, India
where the Buddha attained enlightenment

Right now is one of the very beautiful moments in our lives. We're activating and glorifying our innate beautiful nature of love, kindness, and compassion. Therefore, bring more joy and happiness to yourself, and bring joy, happiness, and peace to all living beings. This is so wonderful! What else is there in the world that's better than this? Think carefully. This isn't just some statement, or something the Buddha said that we should blindly follow. Think carefully. What do the teachings say? "Connect your mind with your heart, and reflect on whether it's true or not." What else are we doing? This is what we're all doing according to our best capabilities—with devotion, joy, and love. We're working to bring peace, harmony, and happiness to ourselves and to all living beings.

We're also trying to remove and release the hindrances and obstacles that are blocking these beautiful qualities. That's what we've been discussing and practicing, and that's what the Buddha taught. We're following the voice of the lineage masters. This is wonderful! What could be better? There's nothing more important than this in life—or even beyond this life. So bring joy and peace into your heart.

Why do we keep creating darkness in our hearts and minds? Why are we spoiling our lives? We've already spoiled things enough. We've been carried for so long by the forces of duality, ego, doubt, hesitation, and skepticism. According to the Buddha's teaching, this has been going on for a *very* long time—since beginningless time. Now we have to say, "Enough is enough." We're in America, so we have to follow the American rhythm and say, "Enough is enough." Truly, I'm not just making some casual statement.

If we want to be kind, good, and make something meaningful out of our lives—to really change our state of mind and bring sunshine into our hearts—we need to bring up more joy, peace, and happiness in our minds. Also bring up more bodhichitta thoughts that are full of love, kindness, and compassion for all living beings—not just self-centered mind. We've been thinking of 'I,' 'I,' 'I,' for a long time. The great master Shantideva said, "We've been practicing self-centered mind since beginningless time. But how much have we achieved? How successful have we been?" On the other hand, look at the example of the Buddha and all the great bodhisattvas. They put all sentient beings in front of themselves, and what did they achieve? They were full of joy, love, kindness, and respect and appreciation. They were so down-to-earth—not hovering in the sky, following after this and that. Read about their actions and legacies. Read their life stories—those are great teachings on bodhichitta, love, and kindness. Similarly, we're trying to activate ourselves and follow in their footsteps. What could be better or more beautiful than that? Think about this.

Of course, there are so many things in samsara that we could do. These are called the "five sense pleasures" of beautiful forms, sounds, smells, tastes, and sensations. How much pleasure, happiness, and peace do these things really give us? Look for yourself. This is one of the most beautiful and richest countries in the world, and we've all enjoyed pleasurable experiences to some degree—how much joy, peace, and happiness did they really bring us?

Many times people have to rely on drugs because they feel that what they have isn't enough, and then it ends in disaster... all because they didn't illuminate their inner heart of joy, peace, and bodhichitta. On the level of samsara, they had the utmost supreme quality of the five pleasurable objects, yet still they weren't fulfilled. We hear about this happening all the time in the news. Compared with that, what we're doing here is so special. So bring up more joy and peace. This isn't joy, peace, and happiness that comes from arrogance. I'm talking about joy and peace that is humble and simple, and filled with great confidence. Great self-contentment. In Buddhism—or by any standard—this is what makes a meaningful life.

Together with this, we are studying and practicing *Vajrayana*, and particularly *Dzogchen*. In reality, everything is already enlightened in the state of the *three kayas*. Our own experience of this is spoiled only by duality, grasping, and clinging. Today we would like to remove, release, and liberate that duality and reveal the way things are in reality. Open your windows and doors and allow that realization to shine! Don't leave it covered by the thick ice shield of grasping and duality. Open up! Activate your realization so that everything is in the state of purity. Again, this isn't just some casual statement. In reality, this is how everything is. We want to open the door and not linger in the deep, dark corner of the duality icebox.

This is known as "practicing." We're practicing goodness—not ego. We're not practicing negative emotions. We're really trying to change our lives and make a difference for ourselves and other beings. That's what it means to be a true practitioner according to the Buddha's teachings. We're practicing very humbly, simply, and down to the ground. Following the advice of the great master Patrul Rinpoche, we're not just practicing "rainbow mouth"— merely talking and paying lip service to the teachings. We need to absorb the teachings into our hearts, and let them grow and shine. That is what practice really is.

Of course we know this is generally the Buddha's teaching, but what is the Buddha's teaching really? If you think about it, what we're really talking about is love. We're talking about kindness and compassion, and about how to remove and release the grasping of duality. This isn't only taught in Buddhism. The nature isn't dominated by any one tradition. The nature is free, open, and relaxed. These different labels are only duality. We fabricated them. Just like the great master Mipham Rinpoche said, we're "trying to lasso and tie up the sky." But of course we can't tie up the sky. Trying to only makes us tired and bored and we're the ones who suffer—not the sky.

We're talking about loving-kindness, compassion, joy, peace, happiness, respect, and appreciation. We're talking about removing all the grasping of self-centered mind. As I mentioned, this isn't only taught in Buddhism; the Buddha simply pointed out the way the nature is. That's why the Buddha said, "I'm a teacher. I'm showing you the nature as it is." This is what the gracious teacher Buddha taught and what he practiced. His actions followed his words. He was humble and simple, and walked with bare feet, holding an alms bowl, carrying his own robes. He walked through cities and villages, picking up his own food along with his students. The Buddha didn't act as if he was a big deal, saying, "I'm the boss," or acting as if he was a big king. This was because of his love, kindness, compassion, joy, and appreciation for every living being.

The teachings say the Buddha loved all living beings like his only child. Truly, this is what the Buddha did and this is what he taught. Love and compassion have no boundaries, none at all. We need to reactivate these beautiful qualities within ourselves. This will make our lives meaningful. We will be happy, peaceful, and joyful in this life, and we will leave this life with joy, peace, and happiness. We will also leave a good legacy and example for our family members, friends, neighbors, and for everyone we're connected with.

CHAPTER 2

THE FOUR NOBLE TRUTHS OF LIFE

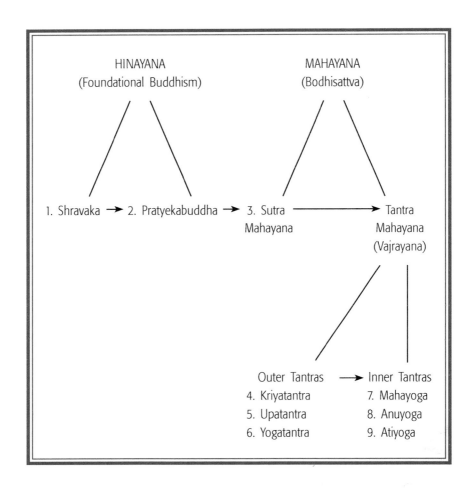

The Nine Yanas

The kind, gracious, and compassionate teacher, Buddha Shakyamuni came into this world and gave many different teachings that expressed that nature of phenomena—the true nature of reality—and dispelled all false images and obscurations. The reason the Buddha gave so many teachings was in order to meet the desires and needs of the variety of individual practitioners. The Buddha gave those teachings according to the different intellectual levels of individuals: some were very intellectually sharp, some were at a more medium level, and some were of lesser intelligence. To suit the different needs of everyone and to bring them the most benefit, the Buddha gave 84,000 different teachings.

Even though he gave so many different teachings, the *nature* of the teachings is the same. The direction the teachings point to is the same because the nature is always the same. There aren't many different natures. Still, all the levels of the teachings can be very extensively categorized or divided into the twelve excellent spoken teachings. Those twelve excellent teachings can again be condensed into what are known as the *nine yana* teachings, which can be further summarized into the *three yanas* of Foundational Buddhism, Mahayana Buddhism, and Vajrayana Buddhism. Even though there are all these categories and divisions, the nature is still the same. This one nature is known as the great nature of emptiness, or the true nature. For this reason, the Dzogchen *King of Creation Tantra*, or *Kunjed Gyalpo*, said that even though there is only one nature, the techniques to realize that nature appear in nine different ways, which is why the Buddha taught nine yanas.

Still, the nature is the same: great emptiness. It's also known as the "one great sphere," or Dzogchen. Dzogchen is considered the highest teaching, but each teaching leading up to it is part of the foundation of Dzogchen practice. The teachings aren't contradictory, oppositional, or separate from each other in any way.

What is the Dharma? What's the purpose of all these teachings? We should always think and reflect on that. The purpose of the teachings is to dispel negativity, and the root of negativity is ego-clinging. Ego-clinging is surrounded by many emotions, such as attachment, anger, jealousy, hatred thoughts, arrogance, and skepticism, or doubt and hesitation. All of those negative emotions support ego-clinging and are a hindrance to ourselves and others. They're troublemakers—obstacles that spoil everyone's nature, including our own. In other words, they spoil our joy, peace, and happiness and they constantly create troubles and obstacles for us. That's why the Buddha used the metaphor of poison for the three or five primary negative emotions of ignorance, attachment, anger, jealousy, and arrogance.

All of these poisons only bring more and more poison. Attachment brings more attachment, anger brings more anger, and the consequence is always pain, suffering, and sadness for oneself and those around you. They spoil our path, our goal, and our vision. And they don't just spoil things in a small, localized way or for a short time—their effect is huge and wide, ruining things now and long into the future. The Buddha taught that the negative emotions are a direct passage to the three lower realms. Basically this means that negative emotions continuously bring negative consequences, spoiling all our joy, peace, and happiness.

The Buddha didn't say that we have to accept this teaching on blind faith. We can look and experience this for ourselves. Negative emotions are obstacles that destroy our present joy, as well as our permanent future joy. That's why we practice the Dharma. Dharma is the antidote. Dharma is the technique or method that will ease negative emotions now, and with continued practice, it will completely uproot them so they no longer disturb us or any other living beings, and no longer interrupt our future destination. That's why Buddha Shakyamuni taught the Dharma and it's the purpose of meditation practice.

Why is it that these poisons are constantly making so much trouble? Why are they such a pain in the neck? Because they aren't natural. They're delusions. They're obstacles and we get so carried away by them—that's why they're so problematic. What is the opposite of delusion? The true state of egolessness. Egolessness is natural. When you rest within the state of egolessness, you're resting in the true nature.

We're always talking about bodhichitta: love, compassion, wisdom, joy, and appreciation. Why do we emphasize this so much? Because these qualities *are* the nature of your mind! When you're with the nature, you always feel good because it's natural! You're connected to what is natural. What is the opposite of anger? Love. True love is the natural state of the mind, so it brings more joy, peace, and happiness. In the West they often use the expression "home sweet home," which means that you feel the happy, joyful state of returning back to where you belong. Similarly, when you're in the state of loving-kindness, compassion, wisdom, joy and appreciation, you feel very calm, peaceful, and kind of homey. You feel very natural. It's soothing. When you're in that natural state, it's not only you that feels it—your energy spreads out to others, including your friends and family members. Then you bring that energy to others, and that's how you can create peace and happiness for others. That is known as being a bodhisattva.

For these reasons, the gracious, kind, and compassionate Buddha gave his first teaching in Varanasi, India. This first teaching he gave is known as the *Four Noble Truths*. In this teaching, the Buddha gave a general explanation of the truth of reality as it is. That's why it's called "truth," because the Buddha didn't create, exaggerate, or deprecate anything. He explained the truth simply as it is, and therefore it is known as "noble." He wasn't trying to create excitement or stir up any emotions—he was simply explaining the truth as it is.

The first two truths are known as the Cause of Suffering Truth and the Suffering Truth. In Tibetan, the Cause of Suffering Truth is known as *Kunjung Gi Denpa*, which means "source of everything." In English, it's usually translated as the "Cause of Suffering Truth." The cause of all suffering is ego-clinging and negative emotions. Ego-clinging is the source of every trouble, and the three or five poisons are like the ego's retinue and act as the principal supports of ego-clinging. Wherever we go and whatever we do, negative emotions and negative activities together create *karma*. These negative emotions and activities are the source of every trouble. They follow us like a shadow. Therefore, Buddha named them as the source of everything in samsara.

The result they bring is the second truth, which the Buddha called the Truth of Suffering, or *Dugngal Gi Denpa* in Tibetan. Suffering comes whether we want it or not. When causes and conditions come together, there's no way to avoid the result. The result is right there. When there is a body, there is always a shadow—it doesn't matter whether you want it to be there or not. Similarly, when the causes of suffering such as negative emotions and ego are there, the result of pain, suffering, and all the difficulties of samsara come along with that package. We can't separate them. Even if we don't want it to be that way, the suffering will come. We are actually indirectly creating it ourselves because the ego and negative emotions are the engine, producer, and manufacturer of this suffering.

A simple way to explain or summarize the Suffering Truth and Cause of Suffering Truth is samsara. The cause of suffering and the suffering itself—both are nothing besides samsara, or the world. Generally speaking, where does samsara come from? Where is it produced? It is self-created by our own deeds. It is ego-clinging. It is negative emotions. Samsara isn't some other place out there that we project or look at. Samsara is engineered, produced, and accelerated within and by one's own self. That is a simple way to explain it.

The gracious teacher Buddha pointed out that samsara is the ego, negative emotions, and their result. That is samsara. If we'd like to avoid samsara and not experience so many difficult situations, then we can apply the techniques that the Buddha explained in the third and fourth noble truths, which are known as the Path Truth and Cessation Truth, or *Gokpai Denpa* and *Lamgi Denpa* in Tibetan.

The noble Path Truth is practicing the opposite of negative emotions and ego-clinging. When we perform activities that are the opposite of ego-clinging and the opposite of attachment, anger, jealousy, hatred thoughts, ignorance, doubt, and hesitation, that is known as the noble Path Truth. What are those activities? As we've been discussing, and as we're all trying to practice, these are known as love, compassion, wisdom, joy, appreciation, non-attachment, and nongrasping. Dzogchen meditation or any meditation practice is the noble Path Truth. All practices that are based on loving-kindness, compassion, joy, devotion, and appreciation—whether you're practicing *Vipashyana* or *Shamatha*, *Visualization Stage* or *Completion Stage*, Dzogchen or *Mahamudra*, whatever you practice—if it's based on those beautiful thoughts and motivations, and your practice develops alongside them, this is known as the noble Path Truth.

Another simple, everyday way of describing the Path Truth is going against ego-clinging and negative emotions. According to Dzogchen, you transcend, transform, or liberate ego-clinging and negative emotions into their own natural state. You're constantly coming back to your own true nature, dispelling all negativities. That is a simple way of understanding the practices of the noble Path Truth.

According to the Buddha's first teaching, continually practicing and following the Path Truth will bring the result of the noble Cessation Truth. In Sanskrit, the word 'cessation' is *nirodha*, and in Tibetan it's known as *gokpa*, which means "negation" or "ceased." What has ceased? Negativity and ego-clinging are completely finished. When ego-clinging and negativity no longer arise, both the cause and results of samsara are exhausted. You are free from samsara and its consequences.

CHAPTER 3

DISCOVERING
A RELIABLE REFUGE

First Buddhist Council

In Buddhism, the general objects of refuge are the *Three Jewels*—
the *Buddha, Dharma,* and *Sangha.* This is true for all the schools
of Buddhism, including the *Hinayana, Mahayana,* and the
Vajrayana schools.

THE BUDDHA

Buddha is a Sanskrit word, which means "totally awakened" or
"enlightened." It is the state of unconditional love, compassion, and
wisdom. Buddha can also be understood in terms of the three
kayas. *Kaya* is a Sanskrit word that means "heap," "compounded,"
or "body;" it refers to the marks of enlightenment. Of the three
kayas, *dharmakaya* is the absolute state of the true nature. It is
without form and is the ground, origin, and source of everything.
Sambhogakaya is the clarity or energy aspect of the true nature—
its power and creativity. *Sambhoga* means "enjoyment." An
enlightened being does not accept or reject, but rather enjoys all
things. *Nirmanakaya* is the emanated or manifest body. It is the
activity of enlightened beings that reaches out to all sentient beings.

According to the Mahayana teachings of the Buddha, once you're
free from samsara and its consequences, that is known as reaching
enlightenment. You become a buddha, an awakened one. You have
achieved the dharmakaya, sambhogakaya, or nirmanakaya state of a
buddha, or reached the realization of a buddha. All of these different
terminologies mean that your ego-clinging and all negativities have

completely ceased, and you've achieved the state of buddhahood, or the three kaya state. Cessation or buddhahood isn't some new thing that comes to us that we don't already have. Becoming enlightened is returning back to our true nature, where we really belong. In other words, we stop clinging to our ego. Attachment ceases, clinging, grasping, and negative emotions all cease, and the moment we completely stop all that, we reveal our innate, inherited nature. That is known as buddhahood, or enlightenment.

The Dharmakaya Buddha is named Samantabhadra, or Kuntuzangpo in Tibetan. This means "All-Good," or "Everything is Perfect." This Buddha is usually depicted as naked to symbolize formlessness and also freedom from conceptions. The sambhogakaya buddhas such as Vajrasattva and the other *Five Dhyani Buddhas* are brightly colored and adorned with beautiful silks and jewels which symbolize the richness and joy of enlightened experience, and the fact that anything and everything can be used as a means to total awakening. The nirmanakaya buddhas often appear as actual human beings in the forms of great teachers. The two leading examples of nirmanakaya buddhas are Buddha Shakyamuni and Guru Padmasambhava.

THE DHARMA

The Dharma, or the message of the Buddha, is that which removes suffering, promotes peace and happiness, and ultimately brings limitless, unconditional love, compassion, and wisdom. The purpose of the Dharma is to uproot, transcend, or liberate our ego-clinging and negativities. Whichever approach we use according to the different teachings of the Buddha—whether we're practicing according to the *sutra* or *tantra* approach, or using Dzogchen techniques—the purpose is the same.

Our own mind is the primary target of Dharma practice. Of

course we have to study and understand the teachings, but the point isn't just to be able to recite something—the Dharma has to be absorbed into our hearts and minds. Dharma isn't a show or some kind of an announcement or proclamation. Of course, we may occasionally announce and show the Dharma, but the essence of Dharma is practice and absorbing the teachings into our hearts and minds.

Let your mind become gentler. Let it be more peaceful and more joyful. Let your mind be full of love, kindness, patience, and understanding. Don't let your mind be restricted by clinging to ego or negative emotions. Don't let it be carried away with skepticism, doubt, hesitation, intellectual ideas, or traditions. This doesn't mean we can't have traditions or these other things, but when we're practicing the Dharma, let them dissolve. Let them vanish within the space of the *dharmadhatu* and bring forth the genuine open, calm state of mind, and relax. Just be in that state. Let joy, peace, and appreciation arise very naturally, like rainbow light or the mists of springtime. Keep this view all the time with the joy of sunlight in your heart and mind. That is known as practicing the Dharma. Really try and focus your mind with mindfulness, joy, and alertness, always trying to bring forth those qualities as much as you can.

THE SANGHA

The Sangha is the assembly of individuals who are devoted to and have confidence in the Three Jewels. *Sangha* is a Sanskrit word; its root meaning is "inseparable" and "unshakeable." This refers to the bond these individuals have with the Three Jewels, and therefore with one another. Sangha members support one another on the path to enlightenment. The sangha can be divided into two major groups: beginners and advanced. The advanced sangha can further be divided according to how far they have traversed the *ten bhumis* or *five paths*. Whether one is a beginner or more advanced, the intention and identity is the same. By taking refuge, one becomes a member of the sangha.

Sangha is a spiritual community—a group that has the power of love, joy, appreciation, wisdom, and great patience. All of these natural inner qualities are arising beautifully like fireworks on the fourth of July, or maybe like something you'd see at Disneyland. These beautiful, amazing qualities are suddenly popping up, and we're showing and expressing that beauty to each other, reminding each other to be in that state, or in that *mandala*. That is known as the noble Sangha, or noble community.

When we accept the Buddha, Dharma, and Sangha as the inspiration and source of our spiritual journey, and practice the teachings with courage and commitment, this is taking refuge in the Three Jewels. By taking refuge in the Three Jewels, we're creating a profoundly positive cause, and if we persevere, the result will be peace, happiness, and ultimately total enlightenment. And with that will come a great ability to help others.

Refuge means to accept the support and guidance of a reliable friend who is also an expert. We sentient beings have dualistic perception and the six poisons that accompany it, and as a result, we experience difficulties and suffering. We seek happiness but find it only intermittently; more often we find frustration and sorrow. If we want this to change, we must find help, just as a sick person must find a reliable doctor. The doctor, in this instance, is someone who has already gone through and passed beyond duality and the six emotions, and who knows precisely what sort of spiritual medicine we need. This person is known as a "lama" or "guru." We must heed the lama-doctor and take the spiritual medicine she or he prescribes for us until we are completely healed. This too is refuge.

What is most necessary for this process to bear fruit is devotion.

Devotion is deep abiding respect, trust, and confidence. The lama is a realized being, full of wisdom and compassion. The lama knows the Dharma, as well as which practices are suited for each student's particular needs and abilities. The lama is a role model and an example of spiritual excellence. For centuries, the teachings have helped countless beings cross over unenlightened existence. We too can cross over—eventually we can become like the lama. As we continue to practice, all of this becomes increasingly apparent, and our motivation to practice grows stronger. Devotion is an enthusiastic commitment to our teacher, the teaching, and to our own path and potential.

The enemy of devotion is doubt. Doubt pervades the samsaric mind. Although it quite often shrouds itself in a seemingly sophisticated intellectual cloak, doubt is nothing other than hesitation caused by fear. Doubt is an expression of nostalgia for samsara. Of the six poisons, it is the one associated with the human realm—our realm. On this journey, we often begin with good devotion, but then doubt arises and we succumb to it. This is a time for courage and commitment. Stay on the path—don't take a detour. Stand up to doubt—don't give in. If we remain steadfast, doubt will retreat as a defeated bully and eventually it will disappear altogether. When doubt is gone, we are firmly established on the path and our success is on the horizon.

The Buddha named three types of devotion: (1) devotion with interest, (2) devotion with desire, and (3) devotion with confidence. These are also known as "interested devotion," "devotion of intense longing," and "devotion of unshakeable certainty." Devotion with interest occurs when we see a beautiful image of the Buddha, encounter the teachings, or meet a master or good practitioner with whom we feel a connection and feel good as a result. Something feels right, familiar—it's as if we're returning home.

Devotion with desire naturally follows. We want to learn more. The more we learn, the more we *want* to learn. We want to enter our home and live there. Devotion with confidence is next. The Buddha, Dharma, and Sangha have become our refuge. Whether we're happy or sad, healthy or ill, or even if we're dying, our devotion and motivation have become unshakeable. We have entered our home, we live there, and we know there is no better place anywhere. At this time the seeds of enlightenment within us sprout and grow lush like a new spring. We are on the threshold of perceiving the infinite purity and perfection of the universe.

Devotion is the precursor to enlightenment. If we don't have devotion, even if we sit with buddhas we won't develop spiritually; the seeds of our enlightenment are as good as burned. For example, Legpai Karma was an ordained monk and a personal attendant of the Buddha, but he had no devotion. In fact, he was critical and skeptical of the Buddha, and thought himself superior. Legpai Karma left the Buddha, went on his own, and spent many years striving for enlightenment, but he got nowhere.

The power of devotion overcomes all obstacles, even time and space. Once the princess of Sri Lanka, Muteg Trengze, heard the name "Buddha" mentioned by a merchant from India. Instantly she was overjoyed and her hair stood on end. She wondered when she would see the Buddha who lived so far away. The merchant told her that the Buddha directly appears to people with strong devotion. She asked, "Will he actually come to Sri Lanka?" The merchant said, "Yes." The princess then asked, "How should I invite him?" "Go to the roof of your palace with flowers, incense, and other beautiful offerings and look toward India," he replied. Say with great faith, "Oh Buddha, great being, for whom time and space are no obstacle, please come here. Your devoted child is calling you to come for her own sake and for the sake of all the other beings who dwell here." The princess did as she was told, and then instructed her servants, "When he comes, you must give him lunch." The Buddha heard her call and said to his students, "I must go to Sri Lanka tomorrow to answer the princess' supplication.

Whoever possesses the power of miraculous travel can join me." Many great arhats joined the Buddha. Together they went to the palace as a flock of swans and greeted the princess.

Devotion isn't for the benefit of the Buddha, Dharma, and Sangha—devotion is for the benefit of the one who feels it. When we reach the third stage—devotion with confidence—the blessings of the Three Jewels enter our hearts and we begin to feel and know the truth beyond concepts. We become strong and joyful. Love and compassion for all beings spontaneously arises. This is why in a sutra Buddha Shakyamuni said, "Oh Shariputra, devotion will bring forth understanding of the absolute truth."

In central Tibet there is a very famous statue known as Jowo Rinpoche. This statue has been an object of veneration for Buddhist pilgrims—masters and ordinary practitioners—since the 6th century. In southeastern Tibet in the Kongpo area, there lived a simple man named Bin. Many people from his region had gone to see the Jowo, and they spoke of their extraordinary experiences in its presence. Bin heard these stories and thought that Jowo Rinpoche was a living master. He thought, "I must see this wonderful teacher," so one day he left. When he arrived at the temple where the Jowo statue was housed there was no one present, not even a caretaker. Bin went inside, saw Jowo Rinpoche, and thought he was seeing a living man. He also saw torma offerings which he thought were food, and butter lamps which he thought were to keep the Jowo warm. Bin was hungry and said to the Jowo that he also would like to eat. He dipped a torma into the lamp oil and ate it. While he was eating he looked up and saw that the Jowo was smiling at him. Bin said, "Even though your food is taken by dogs, you are smiling. Even though the wind blows out your fire, you are smiling. You are a good lama. Please keep my shoes while I do one circumambulation in honor of you." Bin removed his shoes, placed them in front of the Jowo, and did one circumambulation. At that moment the caretaker returned, saw the shoes, and thought, "What a terrible sacrilege!" The caretaker was about to pick up the shoes when the Jowo spoke up, saying, "Don't take those shoes away. Bin from Kongpo asked me to look after them for a few minutes." When Bin completed his circumambulation he put on his shoes and said to the Jowo, "You are a good lama. Next year, please come to my village. I will offer the biggest pig and make the biggest barrel of chang beer. I will wait for you." And Jowo Rinpoche replied, "Yes, I will come."

Bin left and returned home. He told his wife, "I invited the good lama Jowo Rinpoche to our home, so remember to be looking for him around this time next year." The following year Bin's wife was fetching water from the river. She saw something unusual moving in the water and hurried home to tell her husband that perhaps his guest was arriving in the river. Bin rushed to the river and saw Jowo Rinpoche's reflection on the water's surface. Fearing that his lama was drowning, Bin jumped into the river and grabbed the Jowo. The two of them climbed out of the river together. There was a large boulder on the land between the river and Bin's home. Jowo Rinpoche said, "I will stay here instead of going to your home." To this day people go on pilgrimage to the river and the boulder to receive the blessings of Jowo Rinpoche. Everyone agrees that the blessing power of these two sites is equal to that of the Jowo statue in central Tibet. This is the result of Bin's profound, unshakeable devotion. With such devotion, we too can transform the ordinary into the sacred and sublime.

There are three benefits of taking refuge: (1) We will enjoy the best of this life—health, prosperity, and long life. (2) We will be free from ego-clinging and attain great unshakeable peace. (3) We will realize buddhahood, the ultimate state beyond samsara and nirvana.

There are three reasons to take refuge: (1) We want to avoid pain and enjoy pleasure. This is known as the low-level motivation. In Buddhist terms, this is expressed as fearing the lower realms and hoping for the higher realms. The lower realms include the hell, *hungry ghost*, and animal realms. The higher realms are the human, jealous god or *asura*, and god realms. (2) Next, we realize that the three higher realms are in fact part of samsara—they are unstable, transitory, and ultimately painful. We desire to be free from all *six realms* now and want to achieve final peace, or nirvana. This is known the medium-level motivation. (3) Thirdly, we realize that we are not alone. We consider the limitless beings caught in the net of samsara, and with great love and compassion we want all of them to be free from suffering. This is the high-level motivation. Among these three, we must develop the high-level motivation. The merit of this kind of refuge is infinite because the number of sentient beings is infinite. This was clearly stated by the great master Nagarjuna in his text the *Jewel Garland*.

CHAPTER 4

THE FOUR THOUGHTS THAT TURN THE MIND TOWARD THE DHARMA

Four Renunciation Thoughts

In Tibetan, there are two words for renunciation: *ngejung*, which can be translated into English as "renunciation," and then *lodhog namzhi*, which means "four points that will reverse the mind." If we look closely at these words, they really highlight and capture the meaning of what the Four Renunciation Thoughts are about.

The ancient 8th century Buddhist translators in Tibet were also great masters. When they chose certain terms, they didn't randomly create the language using just any words. They really thought and reflected on it using their wisdom, knowledge, and understanding, and then created the various names, titles, and words. Their translations are very special and capture the entire depth of meaning of the original Sanskrit.

Take for example the word *ngejung*, which is translated as "renunciation." *Nge* is a Tibetan word that means "certainly," and *jung* means "renounce." So "certainly renouncing." What does that mean? It means we are certainly uprooting our grasping and clinging, the gluey attachment to this world of samsara. Our attachment is like an octopus. When an octopus catches something, it's very difficult to release. Believe it or not, our attachment is like an octopus. Or it's like glue. I've seen on television that sometimes people shoot glue on robbers so they can't move. That's a very nice, nonviolent, passive way of subduing. Similarly, our attachment is very passive, lurking low in the undercurrents, yet it holds on very strongly. When we reflect on this and have an understanding of the Four Renunciations, that means we're looking closely at the way things are, and where we are.

As Khenchen Palden Sherab Rinpoche and many great masters repeatedly said so many times, our mind is always looking outside—we rarely look inward to ourselves or to the ground where we're standing. In a way, we're always distracted, looking out, out, out. Instead, renunciation looks closely at where we came from, where we are now, and where we're going. We take a panoramic or bird's eye view of our situation and the circumstances of this world of samsara. What happens when we do this? It begins to uproot our attachment. It softens our heart and makes us more practical and knowledgeable, with more understanding of our situation so that we don't keep hovering around, lingering, and ridiculously wasting our time. Instead, we can do something meaningful that reflects goodness in our lives and the lives of others. This is *ngejung*, or *nipar jungwa*. *Nipar jungwa* is renowned terminology used to describe the perfect morality of the great arhats. This is not temporary renunciation, but renunciation that is completely detached and absolutely determined to leave samsara. Renunciation is very important because it makes our heart more soft, kind, and practical. With a softer heart, you naturally begin to feel more appreciation and respect. Life isn't only full of hardships, like running bulls all the time.

The second word, *lodhog*, is translated as "reverse." The meaning is basically the same: reversing our mind from routine habitual patterns. We're always carried away by habitual patterns. However, when we reflect on our situation, it puts the brakes on the habitual patterns that aren't useful or beneficial for us, lowering the speed so we can better understand our situation. By reversing our minds from old, unbeneficial habitual patterns, we can ignite our goodness thoughts, bringing more joy, appreciation, love, and realization. That is really the meaning of *lodhog namzhi* and renunciation: something beneficial that is good for ourselves and others, and it softens our heart.

The Four Renunciations are the essence of the Buddha's first teachings. The Buddha reached enlightenment at age thirty-five. According to the Theravada tradition, he reached enlightenment on his birthday. According to Tibetan Buddhism, he reached enlightenment one week before his birthday party. Either way, it's within a very close range. Seven weeks after the Buddha reached enlightenment, the first teaching he gave was on the Four Noble Truths. Buddha gave this teaching to five human disciples, 80,000 celestial beings, and even many animals came to receive his message.

What are the Four Noble Truths? The first is the Suffering Truth, then the Cause of Suffering Truth, the Path Truth, and the Cessation Truth. The very first message he taught was the Truth of Suffering. What is the Suffering Truth actually? It's a teaching on the way things are in the world, and on renunciation. Next the Buddha taught the Cause of Suffering Truth, because suffering doesn't just erupt without any causes and conditions happening behind the scenes. So the first two noble truth teachings of the Buddha are really on renunciation and the four thoughts that reverse the mind.

The great masters taught by bringing all the practical teachings of Buddha Shakyamuni together into one package. For example, a teaching by Karma Chagme called the *Union of Mahamudra and Dzogchen*, or the *Ngondro* foundational teachings, or even the entire Vajrayana teachings—each of them perfectly combine the natural, organic teachings of the Buddha so that we can easily practice and meditate on them—so that we can actually apply the teachings and practice.

In a way, this first teaching on the Suffering Truth and Cause of Suffering Truth is like an appetizer practice. Many people might wonder why the Buddha taught the Suffering Truth. What difference does it make? Why is this so special? Maybe they think they're just words from La-La Land, or news from Fantasy Island. But the Buddha's teaching is a nugget teaching, close to the way things are, and it's also natural. For this reason, the gracious teacher Buddha Shakyamuni himself said, "I give the teaching. I'm the teacher. I can show you the path, but after that, it's up to you. I can give you every tool, every means to bring yourself up, and then it's up to you whether or not you put it to use."

That's why the first teaching is the Truth of Suffering, or the Noble Suffering Truth. Why is it called *truth*? Because suffering is a truth we all experience. We all go through challenges and difficulties. Nobody can deny or ignore that. It's true, and speaking truth is noble. It's noble because it's spoken exactly as it is—not understated, not overstated, but stated exactly as it is. That is noble. That is beauty. That is special. The Buddha wasn't hiding anything or covering anything up—he was stating the truth simply and plainly, as it is.

So again, among the Four Noble Truths, these Four Renunciations teachings are the first two truths: the Suffering Truth and the Cause of Suffering Truth. They're explained in a very straightforward way so that we can easily highlight them and become more practical. We can soften, have a more tender heart, be more practical and wise, and then, move forward as a nice person, appreciating our own lives and the lives of others.

PRECIOUS HUMAN BODY

The first renunciation thought is about the preciousness of the human body and our life. How rare, how special, how beautiful it is! We have some of the most rare and precious things that are so hard to get, and we have them all at once, in the same place and time. How wonderful! How beautiful! It isn't "co-accidental," or simply casual that we have this body—it's truly our connections and aspirations from the past that are being fulfilled this very moment. We should use the beautiful opportunity we have right now, in every way—in both the worldly samsara way and in the nirvana, or Dharma way. In samsara, we all have everything really. And in the Dharma way, we also have everything. As the great master Karma Chagme Rinpoche points out in the *Union of Mahamudra and Dzogchen*, these are the rarest things! Check for yourself whether this is true or not. We have all the rarest things that Karma Chagme listed one after another:

> There are many aeons, but it is rare for the Dharma to appear. There are many realms, but it is rare for a buddha to come. Although the buddhas appear, it is rare for their teachings to endure. Within the six kinds of beings, it is rare to acquire a human body. Within the four continents, it is rare to be born in Jambudvipa. Within Jambudvipa, the appearance of the Dharma is rare. Even if born there, it is rare to have full faculties. Even if you have full faculties, it is rare to think of the Dharma. Even if you want the Dharma, an authentic guru is rare. Even if you meet one, it is rare to obtain the experiential instructions. Even if you receive them, it is rare to be ripened by empowerment. Even if both come together, it is rare to have a direct recognition of oneself. Your present attainment of all these rarities is not by chance, but by your past prayers. Now is the time to turn your back on samsara! If you are unable to do this, you will be nothing other than someone returning from an island of jewels with empty hands.

We should use this time we have with courage, commitment, joy, and appreciation. Yet this precious situation has the same nature as all phenomena—it's not going to last forever. It's definitely going to change. Everything changes. Nothing lasts forever. For this reason, while the situation is on our side and the circumstances are in our favor, we definitely must use them. We must take advantage. Regardless of whether we choose to use our precious situation now or not, at some point we're going to leave this precious human body. We will have to leave. There's nothing we can do to change course from the rhythm of the nature.

Therefore, take advantage of this opportunity while your body is with you. What should you do with your body? Keep up certain practices; in particular, the great masters say to keep the vows and *samayas* you have received. Keep your vows and samayas clean. To do this, you can highlight the "three vows" of (1) Foundational Buddhism, (2) Mahayana, and (3) Vajrayana. The essence of the Pratimoksha vows in "Hinayana" Foundational Buddhism is renunciation. In addition to renunciation, try to avoid negative activities that hurt yourself or others. This captures the essence of the Hinayana vows. With this foundation, the essence of the Mahayana vows is performing beneficial activities on behalf of others and yourself with bodhichitta. Then in addition to these first two, above that, the Vajrayana vows encourage us to always try to keep pure perception. Another simple way to say this is to have joy, devotion, and appreciation. Feel appreciation for yourself, appreciation for others, and for all situations and circumstances. This is how we can simplify and more practically maintain the essence of the Three Vows.

Next, how can we actually make use of our body, situation, and the time we have? In order to take advantage of having good feet and knees we should do circumambulations, walking around objects of veneration like temples or stupas from right to left, in a clockwise direction. In order to make good use of having beautiful hands, arms, and shoulders, we should do prostrations to objects of refuge. I'm sure you've heard about the many benefits of doing circumambulations and prostrations, so I'm not going to talk too much about it now, but the teachings say they are so powerful.

For example, Buddha Shakyamuni accumulated merit for three countless plus 100 aeons in order to reach enlightenment and become a buddha. Toward the end of his last batch of aeons, as he was activating more and more enlightened qualities, he was born as a Brahma's son during the time of Buddha Kargyal. To show his courage, commitment, strength, and determination, he did circumambulations around the Buddha on one foot nonstop day and night for one week, chanting praises to the Buddha. The teachings say that this activity shortened his last 100 aeons of accumulating merit by 9 aeons! So afterwards, he only needed to accumulate 91 aeons of merit. In Tibetan Buddhism, they still chant these praises. In that simple praise, he said:

> Supreme Lord, there is not another sage like you in the god realm, nor in this world, nor in the land of Vaishravana, not even in the palaces of the gods, nor in any of the four directions or intermediate directions. Even if all the mountains and jungles on the earth were searched, your like would not be found.

That was the essential meaning of his praise as he did circumambulations nonstop for one week.

Next he says we should make good use of our tongue by chanting the six-syllable mantra of the Buddha of Compassion, OM MANI PEME HUNG. We should make use of our illusory wealth and do meritorious activities, such as making offerings and giving generously to others. Make good use of our mind and our intelligence by meditating on the union of compassion and emptiness. Now is the time! We're borrowing this body from the four elements. We don't own it—we borrowed it from the earth, fire, water, and wind elements. We borrowed the solid, fleshy part of our body from earth. We borrowed the warmth aspect of our body from fire. We borrowed the liquid part of our body from water. And we borrowed our breath and air from wind. We will have to give it all back. Eventually, we will be evicted and kicked out. So while this beautiful body is still intact, we should really use it well.

If you use it really well and you take full advantage of your body, then even when you have to give back what you borrowed, it's OK. You can be happy, thinking, "I took advantage of what I had. What I borrowed isn't really working well anymore, so why should I try so hard to keep it up? Why am I worrying about this? Why hesitate?" Be happy to return it back to where it belongs. For example, in ancient times when you had to travel somewhere you would go by horse if you had one. In Tibet if you were traveling and you had yaks, the yaks would carry the luggage. If you didn't have either, you would just walk. But if you did have a horse or a yak and you were going traveling, then you would really take advantage and go forward! In other words, the horses and yaks are waiting to carry you and your luggage, so now it's time to go! You should take advantage. Even if it's a little inconvenient, don't think or feel that way. Take advantage.

Similarly, every situation is in our favor. Every circumstance and condition is going our way. We should take full advantage and be happy. Even when you have to go, just go and do it. Then it's really great! You can feel happy afterward, thinking, "Oh I did it, I got it. I finished and completed everything I could do to the best of my abilities. How wonderful." And then look to the next stage. That's what we should do with this precious human body.

Of all the possible situations we could have, what we have now is so beautiful, so special, and so rare. We should use this opportunity and then we won't feel bad later, feeling guilty about something we didn't do or should have done. We won't be murmuring those things to ourselves later. We just need to take advantage right now of our precious human body and make something special and meaningful with our lives.

IMPERMANENCE

The second teaching of the Four Renunciation thoughts is impermanence. Everything is impermanent. Contemplate this along with the preciousness of your human body.

Of course, we all know that everything is impermanent. That's the nature of everything. There isn't anything unusual about this teaching. Impermanence isn't some kind of Buddhist dogma or strictly a Buddhist idea. It's the way things are. Whether we'd like to accept it or admit it, it's the truth. Everything is impermanent.

There are two levels of impermanence: gross impermanence and subtle impermanence. Gross level impermanence refers to things that most regular sentient beings can easily see. For example, if a building is getting old and falling apart, we might say, "Oh, it was getting old and it collapsed. It's impermanent." Or when something stops working we say, "Oh, it's impermanent. It doesn't last." That's known as gross impermanence which gross mind can easily understand.

The cause of tangible, gross impermanence is subtle impermanence. Subtle impermanence is a chain of instants. For example, when you look at the hours in a day, nine o'clock didn't just happen that moment. It happened after eight o'clock. It keeps on ticking, ticking, ticking. The seconds are moving; second-by-second and then minute-by-minute. It keeps moving. So when we're drinking our eight o'clock coffee, nine o'clock has already begun. It really began right there. These are just examples of subtle impermanence according to time, but everything is involved. Everything begins at the subtle level, even if we don't see it. Mostly we don't see that level, and that's why the great master Buddha Shakyamuni and other great masters often said that the gross mind of sentient beings can't understand or detect subtle impermanence very easily because they're so focused on the gross level. We're always vaguely looking out only at the tangible level. But enlightened beings and great, realized practitioners can immediately understand the subtle instants of impermanence.

The Buddha and many great masters used the example of a hair. You don't notice if a piece of hair falls onto your hand. You don't even feel it. It can just sit there. But if that same hair goes into your eye, you'll notice it immediately. Similarly, the gross mind of sentient beings is so gross that it can't understand these subtle level changes. Yet the realized wisdom minds of great beings are so alert and awake that they know the instant things happen. They realize everything so clearly.

Therefore, impermanence is nature's rhythm. It's nothing new. Everything changes. But when things change, duality mind doesn't like to see it because it's grasping. Attachment doesn't like to see change. When things change on the gross level, we suffer. We feel the impact. In a way, we're almost crushed because the way things truly are is the complete opposite of grasping and duality. So we suffer. Duality beings suffer. Otherwise, it's just change. Things have been changing from the moment we were conceived. We were babies, then infants, teenagers, and now we're adults. It's always been changing, always moving. There's nothing unusual going on, but now we're looking closely to the way the nature's rhythm really is.

Even this planet will change. According to the Buddha's teaching, it will be destroyed by fire, water, and wind that are known as the "fire at the end of the aeon," "water at the end of the aeon," and "wind at the end of the aeon." They will completely destroy this gross world. And of course, it's all already subtly changing all the time—it's not only going to happen at the end of the aeon. When you really look, the world is constantly changing; time is changing, the seasons are changing from spring to summer, winter, and autumn. Just look at one day—from sunrise to sunset, nothings stays the same.

Things aren't only changing on the external level of the world and universe. On the inner level, sentient beings are also constantly changing. If we look to ourselves, from the time of our infancy to being a grownup, there are four primary stages or big changes in life. These are known as birth, getting old, sickness, and death. There are many additional stages, such as decline and other changes we go through, but these are the four biggest transitions, or changes that we all go through.

So what is this impermanence? It's like the ripples of a lake, constantly coming, one after another. It never stops changing. The moment something appears, that very same moment it's changing. In Buddhist philosophy, these are referred to as "compounded" things. Compounded things change the moment they arise. The moment something is there, right that second, it's changing. It also means that it can only be there in the first place because of change! The moment there's matter or mass, right that moment, it's changing or transforming, again and again. Therefore nothing is permanent.

The Buddha's teachings mention four types of endings: (1) things that are erected will fall down in the end, (2) things that come together are going to depart, (3) at the end of birth is death, and (4) the end of growth is decline. All things that gather together or connect will eventually come apart in the end. Everything is like this.

This isn't only true for sentient beings. Even for great beings like Buddha Shakyamuni and all the enlightened beings who completely transformed everything into the state of great equanimity—on the relative, surface level, even they left. All the sages and masters who could change fire into water and water into fire, who could transform many things into one thing, walk through walls, or fly in the sky—when you read the life stories of all the ancient great masters, in the end, even they had to leave. Even they changed. It's natural. Nothing is permanent. Also the great powerful beings like Brahma, Indra, universal monarchs, and the great kings of the East or West, great warriors, or the wealthiest beings in the world— when you look, they all had to leave. Even very powerful beings who scare others simply by hearing their names—even they have to go. Rich or poor, there's no exception. When we look closely, that's just the way things are.

Also, there are so many obstacles to life. For example, the Buddha and many great masters often said that life is like a little butter lamp in the wind—any moment it can blow out. Or it's like a little water bubble on a wave—it can burst at any moment. There are many unfavorable connections, and even the connections we think are favorable can sometimes turn out to be completely opposite from what we first thought.

In the Buddha's teachings, and also in Tibetan Medicine texts, there are 404 different diseases that are the principal unfavorable obstacles to our health. The first are related with the three elements of the body: phlegm, bile, and wind. There are 101 diseases related with bile, 101 diseases related with phlegm, 101 diseases related with wind, and 101 diseases related with some combination of them. There are also many karmic diseases, as well as about 80,000 obstacles that could occur suddenly even if our phlegm, bile, and wind are in perfect balance. In this way, our life is very precious but also very fragile, like a flame in the wind. When will this fragile life blow away?

When I was young, my father Lama Chimed always used to chant these prayers and statements. I always wondered, "Where is he getting these? Where did they come from?" Later on he showed them to me in Karma Chagme's *Union of Mahamudra and Dzogchen*. These are very powerful images and examples that are so easy to understand and clearly show us how life is, and how it's going to end. Life is the same as a prisoner going to a place of execution. A time will come when no medicine can help us, and no prayers will prevent our death. When will that time come? When is this life going to end? The time is going to come, just as the sun always sets behind the western mountains. No one can pull back the setting sun. This is how impermanence is.

Even if you have many wealthy relatives, or many retinues and friends, there isn't a single person or thing that we can take with us. Even if you have incredible wealth, you can't take any of it with you. When it's time to leave, you will have to leave alone. When will this time come? Will you recognize your last moment when all the gross elements are dissolving, and then when the final subtle elements dissolve and different signs appear? When will this moment come? Again, this process doesn't just happen for a few people. Everyone has to go through these stages, one after another.

The moment after we die, all the different visions of the peaceful and wrathful deities will come with loud sounds and beams of light. When exactly will those come? And when will the different experiences of the bardo come? At that time, even if you want to do something about your situation, even if you feel regret, thinking, "I didn't take advantage of my opportunity," by that time it will be too late. At that point, nothing can change what's already started happening. Therefore, we should use this beautiful opportunity we have right now. We shouldn't deceive ourselves. We should be practical and not fool ourselves, or fool around with the time we have.

SAMSARA IS SUFFERING

The third renunciation is to deeply contemplate how samsara is full of trouble. According to the Buddha's teaching, there are six realms: (1) the hell realm, (2) the hungry ghost realm, (3) the animal realm, (4) the human realm, (5) the asura realm, and (6) the god realm. Each of these six realms has so many troubles, one after another.

If you'd like to read more about the realms, the *Words of My Perfect Teacher* has many details. According to the Buddha's teaching, there are sixteen principal hell realms and two sub-hell realms, which all together makes eighteen hell realms. The first hell realm is known as the hot hell realm. If a little sparking fire ever touches our flesh, we immediately feel so uncomfortable. We almost can't bear it. But the heat of the fires experienced in the hot hell realm is seven times more powerful than the heat of fire here. Then there are the cold hells. In the wintertime here, for example, we might have one night or a few days of cold and we feel so cold we almost can't bear it. We can't stand it it's so cold. But in the cold hell realm, their cold is seven times more icy cold. Thinking of this we should try to make our lives more meaningful.

The beings in the hungry ghost realm experience thirst and hunger all the time. For example, when we do the Nyungne practice of the Buddha of Compassion, we do one day of fasting and silence. After just one day of fasting here, people will often say they feel dizzy. In the hungry ghost realm they go for many years without food or drink! If we were in that situation, what would we do if we can't even bear one day of fasting and silence now?

The next realm is the animal realm. When lay Tibetans get angry, in colloquial Tibetan they'll commonly say something like, "Oh, that old dog," and they start to pull up on their sword. They say, "That old barking dog," or "that old dog is bothering me," and they pull up their sword like they're going to kill and eat the dog. If you were that old dog, what would you do? Think about the many kinds of troubles that animals experience.

Next is the asura realm. Here if enemies are attacking you, you can run away and escape. You could try to hide or even try to completely avoid the situation. But if you're born in the asura realms where there's constant fighting, you can't just get away. So what would you do? There's nothing you could do to change it— you would just have to continue on like that for a long time. Think of this. The suffering of the asura realm is always like this, full of constant fighting and quarreling.

Next, the primary trouble of the god realm is called "falling down and transferring." For example, here you might be concerned with the position of where you're sitting, thinking, "Oh, I'm not sitting in a good place." This is particularly true in Tibetan monasteries. They always have two seating systems—in the West, they have these two systems as well—the reserved places, and then the rest are first-come, first-served. This isn't just a Tibetan custom—in the Buddha's teaching, most people like to sit closest to the shrine or to the teacher. But particularly for those people who have reserved places, if somehow they end up not having a reserved place, they feel upset. They say, "Oh, I'm not sitting in my posted place," and they feel very uncomfortable. They think, "Oh, I'm sitting in the wrong place," or "they put me in the wrong place. I should be in some kind of honored position." So that's the example—if you feel that you're sitting in a lower place or position, you may feel a little tormented by that. But if you had to go through the experience of falling and transferring like they do in the god realm, then what would you do? That is much more severe, and so much stronger.

The Buddha taught that the god realm is so pleasant all the time. Everyone's always happy and everything is good and convenient. Everything is so beautiful. Then suddenly, one week before a god is going to die, signs come and they begin to realize for the first time that they're going to die. For example, gods don't sweat, but one week before they die, they start sweating. They also don't smell, but now they start sweating and smelling. Their flower ornaments are always fresh and never wilt, but now all their flowers and ornaments begin to decay. Their bodies are always very youthful, but now they see their body aging. Because of these experiences, all of their friends and playmates start distancing themselves. It's almost like when you end up being forced into a nursing home. Everyone is rejecting you. The teachings say that their friends will even come and try to console them, saying, "Oh, it looks like now you're going to leave our world. I wish you the best. Do good things in the human world so you can come back to us."

In addition to this, the gods who are going to die and change their status can very clearly see the future destination of where they're going to take rebirth. The teachings say that the situation the gods experience when they transfer and fall is so severe and tormenting that it's almost not worth being born in the god realm in the first place. Just before transferring they were so perfect and beautiful. However, one week in the god realm is not like one of our weeks—it lasts for a much longer time. That one week for them is so severe, so strong and uncomfortable, and really so upsetting. Transferring and falling down is the suffering of the god realm.

So if you're simply sitting in a lower seat or an unimportant place and you can't bear it since it's so uncomfortable and agitating, then just imagine if you had to go through the falling down of the gods. What would you do?

In the human realm, the biggest troubles we go through are birth, getting old, sickness, and death. In addition to that, there are the troubles of being separated from something that you want. Your wishes aren't being fulfilled. And the physical condition of the human body is always uncomfortable. This is all the result of the Cause of Suffering Truth. The Cause of Suffering Truth itself is uncomfortable, therefore the result is uncomfortable. It's always difficult and uncomfortable, no matter what you do. Even if you sleep on the softest bed, still it's not comfortable because you have to keep turning your body back and forth. And then sometimes you might like to sleep on a harder bed, but even when you sleep on that, it's also not so good. Whatever you do, you're always uncomfortable.

These are the troubles and challenges of the six realms. The six realms aren't just for certain designated people; they are the wandering home for every one of us. After this life, we'll each go to the realm that matches whatever causes and conditions we've gathered in our lives. So now is the time to restrengthen our courage and commitment.

Among the Four Renunciations, or the Four Thoughts that reverse the mind from samsara, this is the third: samsara is full of suffering and difficulty. No matter where we go in the six realms, there's so much trouble. These difficulties are deeper than the ocean and vaster than the sky. In order to avoid this, and to ease our situation and change course, what can we do? We should take the medicine of virtuous activities. Take Dharma as medicine. And we should recognize all unvirtuous activities as poison. They're not correct, and they're not good for us. Of course we know this: poison isn't good for us, and the right medicine is good for us. Therefore, avoid the poison of the unvirtuous, and always connect to the medicine of Dharma. Always have confidence and trust in the Three Jewels of the Buddha, Dharma, and Sangha.

KARMA

The fourth renunciation is that causes and conditions lead to results that are inevitable. In other words, the law of karma is infallible. The first three renunciations of the precious human body, impermanence, and that samsara is full of suffering are all included in the Suffering Truth. The fourth renunciation on the inevitability of karma is the Cause of Suffering Truth. In this way, the first two truths of the Four Noble Truths are principally teachings on these Four Renunciations.

The great master Karma Chagme talks about karma by giving the example of a family. Children born into the same family are always different from each other. Their status, activities, ways of thinking, and their careers are all different. Their life spans are also different. Why does it happen like this? The children have the same parents, and these days it might even be said that they share the same genes and DNA. So how can they be so different? Karma. There are causes and conditions that bring this about— some things we can see, and other things we can't even detect. Yet nothing happens accidentally by itself. Everything comes about through causes and conditions.

This is particularly easy to see on the external level. Nothing happens by itself. We know that. Farmers know that. That's why throughout the centuries and ages, farmers around the world have planted seeds. They know that when they plant a certain seed on the right farmland, it's going to bring about a certain result.

On the internal level, it's the same. Nothing happens by itself. Everything has causes and conditions, which reflect as different results. Who creates karma? Karma doesn't come from somewhere outside. The creator of karma is one's own mind. One's own mind is the creator, producer, fabricator, and also maintainer of karma. Mind does everything.

There are three principle types of karma: positive, negative, and neutral. All of these start with the mind. If you look to your own mind, you can see this. You have positive states of mind, negative states of mind, and neutral states of mind. When the mind is sizzling in the state of emptiness, negative mind states start out just like a hurricane. When a hurricane starts in the Pacific Ocean or off Africa, first tiny, seemingly insignificant things happen right there that later become the causes and conditions to make the hurricane become bigger and bigger. Then wherever it hits there is destruction. Similarly, negative mind starts in small ways that we may not even notice until it ignites and suddenly bursts out. Where does it burst out through? It manifests through the two channels or doorways of body and speech. Whose body and speech? Our own mind ignites the negativity, which later comes out through our body and speech. According to the degree of force or power of the karma, that negativity can become like a strong wind, hurricane, or cyclone that bursts out through our speech and physical body.

The body and speech are an avenue for good, bad, or neutral actions. They are the doorway, and mind is the principle doer. Mind is the engine, the powerhouse. What's the environment of negativity like? It's uncomfortable, it's disgusting, and it disturbs us along with our whole mental state. When that disturbance or poison comes out through words or physical actions, what does it do? It disturbs others too. Because it's a troublemaker! It's like a hurricane. It personally disturbs the person who initiated it; they're not in a peaceful, happy state of mind—that's why it started in the first place. Then the negativity projects outwardly and disturbs others. And it doesn't end there! That's just how the trouble gets started! It ignites and begins to multiply, which is the beginning of negative karma.

Again, what is negativity? You already know this: negativity is ignorance, attachment, and anger. These are the three components of negativity. Ignorance, attachment, and anger are all uncomfortable and harmful. Their combination is not good. They're not good to begin with, and they're not good when they come out in our actions.

Karma is the same as planting a seed on farmland. For example, when you plant just one orange seed and it's properly preserved with causes and conditions, when it blooms, how many oranges come from just one seed? Hundreds of oranges come. Thousands of oranges might even come, one after another. It's the same with karma. If we don't take care of negative karma at the beginning, it multiplies in an unending ripple effect.

It's similar for positive karma. Karma begins with mind—our empty mind is the doer of everything. Positivity starts from our mind. It's like sunshine, or heaps of light in the sky. At dawn, we can see a small amount of light, but then it becomes bigger and bigger until the sun clears away all the darkness. Positive karma is similar. It begins with virtuous thoughts like wisdom, non-attachment, love, and compassion. For this reason, the great master Nagarjuna, as well as Khenchen Palden Sherab Rinpoche always quoted the Tibetan phrase, *"Machag medhing timug mi, dechi leni gewa yin,"* which means having no attachment, hatred, or ignorance, and performing activities from that state of mind. That's positive. When positive mind shines and comes out through your body and speech, it's like sunlight. It lights up your whole system, brain, heart, and body—everything is in a very calm, soothing, happy state. When that energy comes out through your body and speech, it makes others happy too. They feel joyful, peaceful, and good. That is positive karma, and it also multiplies.

What is neutral karma? Neutral means neither negative nor positive. These are casual activities, like looking up in the sky, or just looking into space, or doing something without a specific mental attitude. For example, when you get a glass of water or tea, or do some activity that has very little effect on yourself or others, your mind stays calm and peaceful, but it's in a very neutral, often dull state. So the initial karma is small and has less effect. On the other hand, positive and negative karma are both strong. We can see this for ourselves. When we're in a state of heavy duality with strong ego-clinging, we perform activities that are more negative than positive.

The teachings say that the great ancient Kadam masters—as well as great masters from all the schools—used to look back at the end of each day and count how many positive and negative things they had done. They'd compare and think, checking each of their activities and looking at whether they were good or bad. Karma takes time to mature. If we're talking about negative karma—and in samsara there is more negative karma—that karma is not usually going to mature immediately. It takes time. Just like when we plant a seed, the plant doesn't come immediately. It takes time to mature. Similarly, the result of karmic causes and conditions often take many lifetimes to mature. The teachings say that the result of very powerful karma occasionally comes in the current lifetime, but mostly it comes in future lives.

Whatever the duration, karmic results are inevitable. The Buddha also taught that karmic results can't be transferred, shared, or lessened. They always come back to the doer him or herself. Also, the doer won't experience karma in a vague way. Whether it's good or bad, it comes clearly and will be experienced fully with all our senses. For this reason, Buddha Shakyamuni said that water doesn't experience karma. Fire, wind, and earth don't experience karma either. Karma is fully experienced only by the one who originally created it, however heavy that is.

That's why it's always so important to be thoughtful and take care. We should try to perform even the smallest virtuous actions. That's the starting point. We shouldn't ignore good actions, even if they're small. Similarly, even if something seems like a small negative action, we should pay close attention and avoid it. Many times the great masters—and I remember Khenchen Rinpoche would always say this—that even the smallest sparking fire can burn a whole valley, and the drops from a small leak can fill a whole pot. We shouldn't ignore anything. That's what it means to be thoughtful. Be practical and thoughtful, and think good things. If you see something that isn't very good, the moment you notice it, immediately purify it.

What can we do with negative actions? We can purify them. The teachings always say that negativity has no good qualities, but that its best quality is that it can be cleaned. We can purify the stain until it is entirely removed. If we notice something negative, we should clean and purify it using meditation and the Vajrayana techniques we've learned.

Similarly with the smallest good activities, we should enjoy them! Appreciate the good and increase your joy and devotion. Pray, "Tomorrow may I be able to do even better than what I did today." It's wonderful to highlight our positive actions, and to rejoice in the positive actions of others.

In summary, to activate our practice, we should always remember that life is impermanent. It's important that we take full advantage of this life while we have every beautiful opportunity and everything is in our favor. We should make this life beautiful. Of course in life there are so many chores and things to do. We always think, "Oh, I have to do this chore, and then after that I'm going to do this," but so many people have these same thoughts and end up not doing anything for themselves, and then they have to leave suddenly. That could happen to us too. Therefore, remember: time is precious. This situation is precious. Be practical. Be wise. Do good things. The great master Karma Chagme said that at least three times a day we should reflect on how everything is impermanent. It will make our heart soft. And it will make us more practical.

My father wrote out in his own hand some small quotes and glued them on the surface of his cupboard next to where he practiced. They say: "Life is impermanent, don't waste it."

CHAPTER 5

BREAKING THE CYCLE OF SUFFERING: THE TWELVE LINKS OF INTERDEPENDENCE

Wheel of Life

Our gracious teacher, Buddha Shakyamuni taught the twelve interdependent links as an elaborate, detailed way of explaining the mechanics of suffering. If we want to stop the chain of suffering from continuing to cycle, and reverse it, we have to follow a path. This is the Fourth Noble Truth: the Truth of the Path. The path will lead to the cessation of suffering, which is the Third Noble Truth. This is also known as nirvana, or absolute enlightenment.

In order to understand the twelve links of dependent origination, we must clearly see that everything in samsara—both internal and external—is interdependent.

For ordinary beings in samsara, on the inner level, delusion begins with ignorance. Ignorance is the first link because everything that follows is based on it. Karma, consciousness, the body and mind, contact, feeling—all of these follow one after another until it comes to old age and death. The cycle doesn't end with old age and death—the wheel just keeps on rotating, one link after another. There's a painting of this wheel in the main hallway of Padma Samye Ling. It's an illustration of the first two noble truths: the truth of suffering and the cause of suffering.

The first link, which is ignorance, plus the eighth and ninth links—craving and clinging—are negative emotions. The second and tenth links—habit patterns and becoming—are karmas. Negative emotions and karmas are the cause of suffering. The rest of the links (3-7, 11, and 12) are related to the result, which is suffering. These twelve links are a continuous, ongoing activity that builds on itself, going around and around in spirals.

1. Ignorance (Tib. *marigpa.* Skt. *avidya*)
2. Karmic formations (Tib. *duje.* Skt. *samskara*)
3. Consciousness (Tib. *nampar shepa.* Skt. *vijnana*)
4. Name and form (Tib. *ming dang zuk.* Skt. *nama rupa*)
5. The six senses (Tib. *kyemche druk.* Skt. *shad ayatana*)
6. Contact (Tib. *rekpa.* Skt. *sparsha*)
7. Feeling (Tib. *tsorwa.* Skt. *vedana*)
8. Craving (Tib. *sepa.* Skt. *trishna*)
9. Clinging (Tib. *lenpa.* Skt. *upadana*)
10. Becoming (Tib. *sipa.* Skt. *bhava*)
11. Rebirth (Tib. *kyewa.* Skt. *jati*)
12. Old age and death (Tib. *gashi.* Skt. *jara marana*)

(1) The first link, or *nidana*, is "ignorance," and (2) the second is "karmic action" or "activities." This means that by having ignorance, we begin to create different ignorant activities. So, the second link is the activity of ignorance. (3) The third is "consciousness." By performing the activities of ignorance, dualistic consciousness attempts to follow the direction of those ignorant activities.

(4) The fourth link is called "name and form." When our consciousness attempts to follow karmic activities, it begins distinguishing forms and labeling them with names. This includes imagined forms, mental habitual patterns, as well as relatively existing forms. These are what we begin to cling on to.

(5) Creating labels and following after forms leads to the fifth link, which is the "six sense doors." The six sense doors arise and make distinctions between forms, sounds, smells, tastes, sensations, and ideas, which strongly establishes differences between subject and object.

(6) The sixth link of "contact" then occurs as we begin to work

and deal with various systems of subject and objects, and how they contact and interact with one another.

(7) When a sense door contacts its object—such as when eyes meet a visual form, and an eye consciousness arises—the next link is "feeling," or physical sensation. Through contact, a sensation or feeling is produced, which can either be pleasurable, unpleasurable, or neutral.

(8) Once sensation develops, the next stage is "attachment" or "craving." Whether it's good or bad, we're strongly involved emotionally to either continue or stop the physical sensation, which is the cause of attachment.

(9) By developing strong attachment, acceptance or rejection arises. We begin to analyze more deeply, discriminating between what we want to contact or avoid based on the sensations that are produced, which is known as "grasping" or "clinging." If something seems to be good, we accept it. If it seems to be bad, we reject it.

(10) From these discriminations, another kind of possibility is created, which is "becoming." It leads to a kind of rebirth and a further result of our accepting and rejecting, and we're carried along by it.

(11) By the eleventh link, more situations are made possible, and as a result we again take "rebirth" in samsara, or perhaps it brings forth a new situation that will be experienced in our life. This eleventh link is rebirth, or the birth of a new situation.

Once we develop this new situation or take rebirth, eventually the causes and conditions that support it decline, which inevitably causes (12) the twelfth link of "old age and death," which means cessation. A big change will happen.

These twelve links of dependent origination are continuously spinning, going on and on all the time. The first one becomes the cause, and the second link becomes the result. Then the second link becomes the cause, and the third becomes its result. Each link in this cycle leads to the next endlessly, and we continue rotating in samsara with ignorance. Ignorance is the principal support and base of all the other links, spinning them around and around.

In general, all of our activities happen because of this system of interdependent coordination. But if we look at a larger scale, the cycle of these twelve links is generally completed within three lifetimes: our past life, present life, and our upcoming future life. This sequence of lives completes one cycle going around in samsara, which then begins a new chapter.

The way to reverse this entire cycle of suffering is to dispel ignorance. If ignorance stops, the cycle will fall apart. Like a chain reaction, one link after another will collapse. Each link is the result of the one before it and the cause of that which follows. Ignorance is the cause of karmic formations. Removing it will reverse the inner cycle of interdependence. The opposite or antidote to ignorance (*marigpa*) is wisdom, clear knowledge, and understanding of the true nature (*rigpa*). Wisdom is the antidote to this darkness. With the light of wisdom, the darkness of ignorance will be dispelled.

The wisdom of interdependence sees that everything consists of many combinations of factors that are all connected. Nothing is produced or developed by a single entity. Everything comes about by cooperation, naturally connecting, harmonizing, and balancing countless factors to produce a single item. Just look at one flower. There are trillions of conditions that must come together in order for it to appear the way it is. Even the cause—the seed itself—is dependent on so many combinations. The simplest molecule is not a single object, but contains many protons, neutrons, and electrons.

This is known as dependent origination. Whatever is external and internal are connected—they're not two separate entities.

There is no independent object that arises apart from this interdependent network. That is why the Buddha and master Nagarjuna said, "Everything is emptiness." There's nothing that is not empty. Emptiness is open and flexible. It's like the ultimate state of physics, an infinitely vast openness. This is how all variety, change, and movement happen. It's all pervaded by the energy of space. Form itself is also completely empty. There's no solid, separate, or unchanging entity. Every form consists of a massive network of countless combinations. As you go deeper and deeper, the structure and form gradually recede further and further, and eventually just fade away. Then what do we see? There's nothing we can trace. That is the egoless state, or its physical equivalent.

Nagarjuna praises the teaching of the Buddha by saying, "Dependent origination is the precious and profound treasure of the Victorious One's speech. Whoever sees this nature, sees the Buddha." This is the highest, most extraordinary teaching that had never been revealed by any other teacher before the Buddha. It's not only that the Buddha said it and nobody else had; what he realized and taught is so deep and true. He gave us the keys to discover this treasure exactly as it is for ourselves.

At the very beginning of Nagarjuna's *Root Verses on Madhyamaka* [Skt. *Mula-madhyamaka-prajna*], the Buddha and Nagarjuna said:

> Everything that arises interdependently
> Is unceasing and unborn,
> Neither non-existent nor everlasting,
> Neither coming nor going,
> Neither several in meaning nor with a single meaning.
> All concepts and duality are pacified.
> To this teaching, the words of the fully enlightened Buddha,
> We pay homage!

This is what we always chant at the conclusion of our *Heart Sutra* recitation. Nagarjuna is paying homage to the Buddha and his teaching on the twelve links of interdependence. When you have this realization, you're no longer trapped or limited to one state. Everything becomes soft and fluid. The doors open wide, revealing the rising sunshine power in our hearts as we discover the absolute wisdom of the dharmakaya.

CHAPTER 6

JOURNEY TO AWAKENING: THE NOBLE EIGHTFOLD PATH

Progressive Stages on the
Path of Calm Abiding Meditation

What is "Dharma?" Many of you might have ideas about it, and of course we've seen many books that we call "Dharma," but what is Dharma actually? Dharma is true love, true compassion, and true wisdom. That is Dharma. Nonviolence, truth and honesty, simple respect, appreciation, humility—being natural—that is true Dharma, and that is what the nature is. In a way, it seems like something so ordinary, so why do we need this Dharma? Because we sentient beings are dissociated from the nature. We're always looking for something unnatural. We're not doing it intentionally, but due to the way we behave, our habits carry us away from what's natural and move us toward the unnatural. That's really what's happened. When we're carried away in unnatural states, we delude our nature and our beauty, which is the Dharma. Dharma is what helps us come back to our true nature.

Again, Dharma isn't anything strange or far away. Dharma is true love, true compassion, and wisdom. When you have true love, compassion, and wisdom, then honesty, truth, humility, and simplicity all come so naturally. We don't have to make a big effort to get those things. The combination of true love, compassion, and wisdom is known as "bodhichitta." When our hearts are ignited with bodhichitta, a beautiful abundance of honesty, peace, harmony, joy, appreciation, and respect, all naturally come. But when we're not in that natural state, when our beautiful nature of love, compassion, and wisdom is completely covered by unnatural, negative emotions like anger, jealousy, hatred thoughts, arrogance, ignorance, and attachment—then what comes? Dishonesty, disharmony, restlessness, violence, and unhappiness all come so easily. We don't have to make any effort—they just naturally come.

Dharma is our true nature. When we ignite our beautiful qualities, we're keeping the Dharma in our heart. And it doesn't just stay in our heart—it radiates through our voice and through our physical activities, which become so gentle and peaceful, so nice, soothing, and calming. That's really what the Dharma is. So when we talk about practicing the Dharma, it means we're touching the beautiful qualities of our inner nature. When we're chanting mantras, saying prayers, and meditating, we're leading ourselves back to our nature, and revealing and glorifying that nature.

For over forty-five years—from age thirty-five all the way to age eighty-one—the great teacher Buddha Shakyamuni continually gave teachings. What was one of his very first teachings? The Four Noble Truths. We discussed these before, but because they're so important, we're going to briefly review them again. The Four Noble Truths are: (1) the Truth of Suffering, (2) the Cause of Suffering Truth, (3) the Path Truth, and (4) the Cessation Truth.

Why is the First Noble Truth called the "Suffering" Truth? And what is meant by "truth?" For all of us, suffering is a truth. Of course on one level, if we really think about it and look closely, suffering is an illusion. It's very relative. However, even though it's an illusion and even though it's relative, when we're in a state of suffering, suffering is really true for us. We're experiencing it—it's happening to us physically, mentally, and emotionally. For that reason, it's known as truth. Whether it's an illusion, a display, or a mirage—no matter what it is, we're truly experiencing that. Therefore, it is the truth of suffering.

And what is the Second Noble Truth? Suffering doesn't come accidentally or just by itself. It always has fundamental causes and conditions, which is the Cause of Suffering Truth. The way that suffering appears and reflects might seem as though it happens due to external forces. Yet, external forces are only the conditions.

In order for things to develop and grow in the world, two things are involved: causes and conditions.

For example, when we plant a corn seed, the seed is the cause. For it to grow, a variety of conditions are necessary, such as water and soil. When all of the causes and conditions come together perfectly, then corn grows. The harvest comes. Similarly, suffering has causes and it has conditions. Even though externally it may look like it's appearing on its own, according to the Buddha's teaching, the fundamental cause of suffering is negative emotions, including ignorance, attachment, anger, jealousy, hatred thoughts, and arrogance. When something troubles us in our heart, and mind reflects that through verbal or physical action, a reaction takes place. The same ripple effect will eventually come back to us. It doesn't just stop there; it goes deep down and vast. That action comes about by negative emotions, which are the fundamental cause of suffering, and then when the right combination of conditions join together—whether they're external or internal—the result of suffering will definitely come.

What did the Buddha say is the way out of suffering? The Fourth Noble Truth of the Path. The Buddha taught many ways of traveling the path out of suffering, but as a foundation, he taught the Noble Eightfold Path. In order to come out of suffering, our negative emotions must subside. We have to dismantle and disassemble them because they are the troublemakers—they're poison! They are the cause of our suffering and the suffering of anyone associated with us.

It's not just me saying this—we're all intelligent, we know this already. Whenever we act from a negative emotional state, we aren't the only ones who experience the suffering, difficulty, or unhappiness. Whatever degree of negativity we create produces a similar negative effect in the environment around us, affecting our family, friends, neighbors, and our fellow countrymen and women. That's how powerful it is. To clear away and remove that negativity, we have to start with our minds.

Fundamentally everything starts from the emptiness of the mind. It's all activity of the mind. Just like a hurricane begins in empty space, or a tornado begins in the space of an empty sky, when the proper causes and conditions come together, they can become so violent, creating so many disturbances. In the same way, negative emotions are like tornados or hurricanes, creating disturbances according to the degree of their strength. To come out of that, the Buddha said that the noble Sangha should follow the Noble Eightfold Path.

The Noble Eightfold Path is a general teaching of the Buddha. In other words, there isn't any difference between any of the Buddhist schools regarding the Noble Eightfold Path—"Hinayana," Mahayana, and Vajrayana practitioners all apply this teaching. Every practice falls within the Noble Eightfold Path. It's a central column—an essential practice of Buddhism.

First I'll list the names of the eight, and then we'll go into each one in more detail:

1. Perfect view is a noble path
2. Perfect understanding is a noble path
3. Perfect speech is a noble path
4. Perfect activity is a noble path
5. Perfect way of living or livelihood is a noble path
6. Perfect effort or engagement is a noble path
7. Perfect mindfulness is a noble path
8. Perfect concentration is a noble path

These are our practice, our meditation, and our identity. They are how we can bring up the strength and power of our beautiful nature of true love, compassion, and wisdom. That is what the Noble Eightfold Path means. It is our journey. It isn't an external journey that we're walking—this is an inward, spiritual journey.

We're advancing toward enlightenment, discovering the infinite space of *inner* space—not outer space. This noble path is the way and means to discover our inner beauty hiding beneath so many layers of habitual patterns that we've created with our negative emotions.

1. PERFECT VIEW

The first noble path is perfect view. What is the view? Generally, view means understanding things in the phenomenal world exactly as they are—nothing more, nothing less. This is known as view, or we could also use the word 'philosophy.'

According to the Buddha's teaching, the whole phenomenal world is divided into two groups: relative and absolute. Relative is the way things are here—what we can see, feel, and hear. In other words, everything we relate to. They are all things that function. What is absolute? Absolute is the nature of reality—the nature *behind* everything that we see. We can see, hear, and think about the relative, but there's something deeper behind it. It's not just flat—there's a deeper meaning to what we see and deeper meaning to what we hear and think. This is known as the absolute nature— thinking, hearing, and seeing things *exactly as they are.*

In the Buddha's teaching, relative things that we experience are very much like illusions. When we see reality exactly as it is, we realize that it's an illusion, like a bubble or a mirage. It's impermanent. It's like a bubble because it's impermanent. It's like a mirage because it's impermanent. It's relative because it's impermanent. It doesn't last. It won't stay the way it is even for one second. We aren't able to detect it that fast, but in reality, everything is changing and moving forward every instant. *Everything* is moving. Where is it moving? It's moving back to the emptiness nature, which is where everything comes from to begin with. All of this is "relative truth." In Tibetan, it's called *kundzob denpa*, or *samvrti-satya* in Sanskrit. It's all illusion, a display.

It doesn't matter whether we believe this or not; it is the true nature of reality. Everything is illusory. All of our memories, all of our experiences, all our all ideas—everything is relative. Even though it's relative, there are so many beautiful things to see, experience, behold, and appreciate.

An example of beautiful relative illusion is the thinking mind. Mind is so beautiful, so mysterious. It's very esoteric, in a way. It has love, it has compassion, and it has wisdom. It also has all the negative emotions. Where are these things? They're all here, but where are they *exactly*? If we start looking, we can't find any exact location. How wonderful! How amazing! And nothing is crowded! Everything comes from and merges back to the mind. That is the nature of the relative. It's so mysterious, so beautiful, and so infinite.

Within that, we can ignite the good qualities of the *nature* of the mind, such as infinite love, compassion, joy, and appreciation. If we bring these up in our hearts and minds, it is so good. We don't have to worry that they'll be exhausted or that there will be a shortage of true love and compassion. That is the beauty of the mind. When we begin to explore loving-kindness and compassion, even *more* love and compassion come. We aren't going to lose our true love and compassion. As much as we explore compassion, that much compassion comes. As much as we explore loving-kindness, that much loving-kindness comes. As much as we sharpen our intelligence, that much intelligence and wisdom shines. It's as infinite as the brilliant sun! That is the nature of the mind, the nature of the way things are.

If you look, where does everything really come from? A totally open state of freedom. We can't even find a trace of where that beautiful image or quality is coming from.

How mysterious it is! How beautiful! How vast! That's how the nature of this mind is. Therefore, ignite this beautiful understanding clearly and exactly. Thinking of one's own self and of all beings, there is 100% good reason to bring up more love, more kindness, more joy, and more appreciation. It's good for me, it's good for my friends, my family, everyone. Why shouldn't I bring up more love, compassion, and kindness? We're trying to be smart and practical.

This is known as being a practitioner. "Dharma practitioner" isn't a title. It's not a label. Being a Dharma practitioner means touching the inner core of the nature of your mind, which is love, compassion, wisdom, and openness. Anyone who touches to this nature and brings up these qualities—that is a true practitioner, a bodhisattva. That person is on the path to being an arhat, or according to the Vajrayana teachings, a vidyadhara, yogi, or yogini. Seeing the nature exactly as it is and determining: what is a disturbance? What's good for me? What's good for others? What's bad for me? What's bad for others? Seeing that clearly, exactly, and keeping that view with courage and commitment is what is known simply as "view."

There are so many ways to explain and explore "perfect view" according to the various systems of Theravada, Mahayana, or Vajrayana Buddhism. However, it is the foundational teachings that I'm talking about here, where everything begins. Where understanding, knowledge, wisdom, and intelligence shine. We're touching to the core of our nature. We're not looking around somewhere else and missing the point. We are standing firmly on the ground of the nature and exploring the beauty, beholding the panoramic view of the way the nature is. That is briefly the meaning of the view. Maintaining this is the perfect view of the noble path. Keeping this light in our heart and mind is how we begin our spiritual journey.

2. PERFECT UNDERSTANDING

Once you behold and understand the perfect view, keeping that up continually is known as perfect understanding. We don't just have the view once or as an occasional experience. Keeping up this identity continually with courage and commitment, and preserving it—that is the second noble path of perfect understanding. It also means sharing that view according to your understanding—letting others feel and know that. Of course you're not forcing or imposing your view or ideas on anyone—the view is their nature! True love and compassion is everyone's nature! We're helping to reveal their nature, bringing more peace and harmony so that others can also be more beneficial and happy. We all need more confidence, joy, and appreciation in life. Keeping up the view exactly as we behold it is the second noble path of perfect understanding.

3. PERFECT SPEECH

As you maintain that true view and understanding, the third noble path is perfect speech. View and understanding are more related with your heart and mind—discovering and bringing out your inner beauty. When that beauty begins to arise, let it shine beautifully through your speech. Speech is the communication between the visible and the invisible. Mind is something that no one can see except for oneself. We can feel our own mind, but no one else can. Mind is so personal, private, and individual. No one else can experience our mind directly. However, speech creates a link between one mind and another. Through verbal expression, we can pretty much know the minds of others. We can also express our inner knowledge, understanding, and feelings. Therefore, verbal communication or speech is so important. It's a part of all our activities. For this reason, soft speech that is kind, gentle, respectful, and appreciative is so special and unique. That's why the Buddha named perfect speech as the third aspect of the noble path. It makes the path very bright and clear. The quality of the speech determines how it makes everyone feel. If our speech is wholesome, nice, kind, and soft, it makes others happy and brings them joy and peace. If speech is negative, violent, and disrespectful, it makes everyone unhappy and brings suffering.

According to the Buddha's teaching, there are four types of negative speech. (1) The first is deceiving speech, which we normally call lying. This means that the person telling lies is filled with negative emotions that lead to cheating, deceiving, and taking advantage of others. When these emotions begin to sizzle and reflect through the heart and mind, it's known as lying or deceiving speech, which is very negative. In the Buddha's teaching, there are many different ways of lying. For example, lying about your spiritual realization or abilities is so negative that it can cause you to lose all your accumulated spiritual energy. The teachings mention that it depends on the degree of the lie, but deceiving, lying speech can be very, very negative.

(2) The second negative speech is slander, which breaks peace and harmony. Slander is based on jealousy, anger, attachment, or arrogance. Regardless of the negative emotion, slander is when you disturb the peace, breaking the circle of harmony. It's very violent and negative. It disturbs the peace and happiness of others. Therefore slander is very negative speech.

(3) The third negative speech is harsh speech. This is speech that is very vulgar. It may not even involve really big negative intentions. It may just be short-tempered emotions talking with slightly harsh speech. But again, no matter what the intention is, even if it's based on beautiful intentions, whenever others hear harsh speech, it disrupts their peace. It breaks their joy and brings them unhappiness. Therefore it doesn't matter whether our

intention is good or bad—we have to be thoughtful and avoid harsh speech.

(4) The fourth negative speech is gossip. There are many different ways of gossiping, but most of the time it's based on ignorance, attachment, or some kind of jealousy or arrogance. Talking like this distracts others and creates negativity for them. If the gossip is intentionally targeted toward someone else, then it's even worse and brings more negativity. These are the four negative types of speech.

The opposite of negative speech is perfect speech. What is the opposite of lying? Speaking the truth. Speaking honestly. This is known as perfect speech. Instead of slander, we use speech to create friendship, harmony, and peace. That is the opposite of slander. What is the opposite of harsh speech? Speaking softly, politely, and with kindness. Being polite makes you happy and it makes others happy. Just as the Buddha taught: take yourself as an example and act that way. This is a very experienced statement. It's simple, but so profound. Take oneself as an example. Everyone is the same. Everyone likes to be happy. No one wants to be unhappy. I like to be happy, peaceful, and joyful, and others want the same thing. I like to hear soft, polite, nice, and kind speech, and so do others. And then lastly, the opposite of gossip is very meaningful, devoted, uplifting speech.

Knowing these good qualities and engaging our activity with these kinds of speech is what the Buddha highlighted as the noble path of perfect speech. "Noble" doesn't mean that something is standing somewhere as a title, a statue, or some monument. Noble means speaking the truth, speaking softly and gently, and bringing friendship and harmony. These are all noble. They are Dharma practice. Whoever does this is practicing the Dharma. It is meditation because it directly touches our inner qualities and the inner qualities of others.

4. PERFECT ACTIVITY

The fourth noble path is perfect activity. Perfect activity is how we engage in our primary life activities by doing things that don't hurt anyone directly or indirectly, and instead, helping and supporting others as much as we can, directly and indirectly.

Maintaining good qualities in all our activities can be done physically, verbally, and even mentally. There are three principle negative physical activities. (1) First is taking the lives of others. (2) Second is taking the belongings of others that are not openly given or without permission. (3) And the third is sexual misconduct. These are the three negative activities of the body. Instead, we should try to do the opposite of these. Rather than taking the lives of others, help support and protect life. Instead of taking the belongings of others, give generously to those in need according to your capabilities. Instead of sexual misconduct, behave with good manners. These are the perfect noble physical activities of the Buddhadharma.

I already mentioned the four positive verbal activities of speaking honestly, harmoniously, politely, and meaningfully above, so I won't repeat them now.

There are three negative mental activities. The first negative or unwholesome activity of the mind is covetousness—expecting or cunningly thinking about how to get the belongings of others, sincerely wishing for, and trying to grab them. The second is having a violent attitude by thinking about how to hurt others—physically, mentally, or emotionally—in a prearranged or premeditated way. The third is having wrong ideas, which means trying to impose one's own ideas on others, whether it suits them or not, and believing and acting with this blind idea.

What are the opposite of these negative mental activities? The opposite of covetousness is rejoicing! Instead of coveting, think, "Oh, how beautiful that person is! How wonderful that they have that! I wish they could have even more and better! I wish every living being could have that!" Sincerely wish that and rejoice. The Buddha's teachings say that rejoicing is one of the great meritorious attitudes. It's very special and it accumulates so much merit. The Buddha said, "I can exactly count how many drops of water are in the ocean, but I cannot measure the merit of true rejoicing. That I cannot measure." Buddha appreciated rejoicing that much. So rejoice in others. When we see good things they do or have— enjoy! Enjoy that experience.

There's a joke about this: "How many people does it take to change a light bulb in California? They need five people: one person to change the bulb, and four to experience it!" Similarly, when we see the most beautiful things and the people who have them, instead of wanting to have them for ourselves, we should rejoice for them, and in our rejoicing, we experience it! How beautiful! How lucky I am to have eyes that can see these beautiful things! How wonderful to experience these luxuries of the eye! And I don't even have to make any effort to experience and enjoy that beauty! Thinking this way, wish that they enjoy long-lasting beauty and make that as an offering to the buddhas, bodhisattvas, and enlightened beings, praying that by that merit, may all sentient beings be completely freed of poverty and miserable conditions. Really wishing that and engaging in that meritorious activity is the more spiritual way. Then truly you are making it as an offering. The Buddha really emphasized how special this is. You can use it as a spiritual opportunity to completely transform it into something even larger. That is spiritual and noble.

Next, what is the opposite of violent thoughts? Having thoughts about benefitting others, like "I wish I could benefit them and remove their poverty. I wish I could remove everyone's troubles associated with sickness, getting old, and death. I wish to remove the suffering of all people who are dying, one after another." Really sincerely wish this and pray to the buddhas, bodhisattvas, and enlightened beings: "May this happen exactly as I wish." In this way, join your prayers together with the blessings of all enlightened beings and dedicate that directly toward alleviating the suffering of all living beings. No matter what their situation is, every living being on this earth, including ourselves, will one day have to go through the sufferings of growing old, getting sick, and dying. Regardless of what you've seen or heard, we will all go through that. Therefore, sincerely wishing that every living being is completely free from that difficulty and trouble is our practice. That touches to the very deepest meaning of the Dharma. It may not seem like a big fancy thing, but this is the central column of the teachings and practices of Dharma. Thinking this from the depths of your heart is very wholesome. It's truly so special and beautiful.

Third, what is the opposite of wrong ideas? Right ideas. And how do we know what's "right?" Anything that's based on true love and true compassion—something that brings happiness, joy, and peace to others and one's self—that is a right idea. That is good. Apply that according to the best of your capabilities, as well as the readiness of others. Do whatever you can to bring a positive result to others and yourself. Nevertheless, even if something's so special and good, we can't impose it on others. That won't help anyone. Our intention is to help—not impose. So we act according to the readiness of others, according to our capabilities, and we do that with joy, happiness, and delight! That is a right idea, and the right thing to do.

5. PERFECT LIVELIHOOD

I translated the fifth noble path as "livelihood." This refers to the way we sustain ourselves. Due to having a physical body, we all need food and some degree of comfort to maintain a basic level of happiness, health, and beauty. The Buddha said that there is a perfect way to do that. He said, "Oh noble Sangha, the way to maintain perfect livelihood is with not too extreme asceticism, nor too extreme luxury. The middle way is the path of the noble ones." That's what the Buddha said. So, don't be too extreme on any side. Keep it simple, beautiful, and nice, doing however much you need to do to continually keep your engine running and to maintain goodness. For example, even though these days many of us are enjoying so many yummies, the body doesn't need too much. According to the teachings, the Buddha only ate once a day. Many times the Buddha said that the stomach is divided into three portions: one portion is filled with solid food, one portion is filled with liquid, and one portion of the tummy is left empty because it needs room to digest and evenly distribute the food to wherever it's needed. In this way, it's not too overloaded nor is it too reduced. It's in perfect balance. This perfect balance brings clarity to the mind, and light to the body. The situation is similar with clothing. Of course it was a little different in ancient times, but it's pretty much the same today—having too many things is more tiring and more stressful.

The Buddha taught that we should maintain perfect balance according to our country, circumstances, and the situation where we live. Just balanced. Not too harsh, but also not so extreme that it becomes a burden. Sometimes people use the phrase "not becoming a slave to your wealth." We'd like to *use* our wealth, not be a slave to it. That's really a true statement. We'd like to enjoy wealth, not become a victim of wealth. So maintaining a nice, good, and healthy degree of things like food, clothing, and shelter is known as perfect livelihood, or perfectly sustaining the body.

To review, the first two noble paths are view and understanding, which are related to the mind. The second group is speech, engaging activity, and livelihood, which are more related with our physical and verbal activities. The third group begins with joyful effort.

6. PERFECT EFFORT

Joyful effort is a general support for all the other paths in the Noble Eightfold Path. In order to perfectly maintain the five paths we already discussed, what do we need? We need joyful effort. Joyful effort is the engine that will drive us forward. Not only that, but of the eight noble paths, all seven totally depend on joyful effort. It applies to everything. Without joyful engagement, nothing moves. We know that. In the world of samsara, nothing comes to our door without effort. We have to make the effort. But this effort is joyful! We're doing this for a beautiful, joyful cause. The beautiful cause is to bring joy and peace and happiness to ourselves, and to reveal our loving-kindness, compassion, and wisdom. We're also doing this to support others, with the sincere intention to help them. It's truly rewarding. It is joyful. And it's not just for now—we're cultivating a long-lasting, beautiful joy and appreciation. It's very worthwhile to make this effort.

The opposite of joyful effort is laziness, discouragement, and self-blaming. All of these are types of laziness. Even if it looks like we're blaming others, we're mainly blaming ourselves. It's actually our own laziness. To some degree, we're creating a scapegoat—using other reasons and terminology to cover up our laziness. Deep down, that's what we're doing. But we aren't fooling anyone except ourselves. Laziness is one of the major obstacles to accomplishing things, both in the world and in the Dharma. Therefore, restrengthen your courage, commitment, joy, and appreciation, and maintain your vision and goal. How wonderful!

All the buddhas and enlightened beings achieved their goal through great effort and joy. Just read the life stories of those lineage masters and teachers—how much beautiful joyful effort they made in order to become such great masters. They didn't start out as great masters—it was due to their joyful effort that they became great masters and great teachers.

Take for example the life story of Buddha Shakyamuni. The Buddha recounted all his previous life stories, and one after another, he put so much joyful effort into preserving and keeping up his bodhichitta; he continuously worked to help all living beings with so much love, kindness, and compassion. There are so many examples of great masters. Read their life stories. This is not only true in Buddhism, but also in other traditions as well. Read about those great teachers and saints, and how many remarkable things they did in the world. That's how they came to be called saints. They weren't born as saints. Their actions brought that result and now they're known as saints. Read about them—how humble and simple they were; how much genuine humility they had. They're role models for all of us.

And in Buddhism specifically, when you read the life stories of all those great arhats, bodhisattvas, and mahasiddhas, you'll see how humble they were; how simple and down to earth. They never claimed that they were enlightened or any big thing. They were so simple and casual, so humane and so beautiful. On the ground, they mingled with everyone. Yet their courage and commitment, understanding and wisdom were like the sky—matchless! All of those results were brought about by their tremendous joyful effort.

7. PERFECT MINDFULNESS

The next noble path is perfect mindfulness. Mindfulness is what maintains all the knowledge and wisdom that comes from whatever it is you've learned. Even if we're not able to remember all the details, we really have to keep the principle aspects of what we've learned in our brains and our hearts. If we miss that, we lose our practice and the instructions we've received, and our goal is lost. That's why mindfulness is so important. Mindfulness is what keeps our wisdom shining continually. If we don't have mindfulness, it's as though all our knowledge is switched off and everything we've learned goes down the drain. It's like holding water in the palms of your hands. Even though at first the water can fill up in your hands, pretty soon it's going to drip out. It doesn't stay there long. That's similar to not being mindful. You lose everything. The instructions come and then they're gone. Sometimes there's not even a trace left. That's how fast it can happen. So even if you don't remember all the details, you must keep the principle aspects that are most important for your meditation practice and for preserving and igniting your bodhichitta, kindness, love, and compassion. That's what counts.

What else does keeping up mindfulness do? It makes the mind more stable and we're able to remember more. That's part of mindfulness meditation too. Mindfulness also makes your meditation practice progress well. You're able to see more of what's going on in your brain, as well as with your verbal and physical activities. In a way, mindfulness is like radar. You're continuously checking up on your own behavior. Most of the time we sentient beings are watching others. We seldom check ourselves. Our every focus—almost every one of our senses—is constantly directed externally. But with mindfulness, our knowledge is shining and we begin to check our physical and verbal activity, as well as our way of thinking. That is wisdom.

Mindfulness is wisdom and intelligence. It's very practical. If we have even a little bit of mindfulness, then our behavior will improve. We'll be very thoughtful of the ways we act. We can catch ourselves, thinking, "Oh, I don't want to do that because it will hurt me and it will also hurt others. Why would I do that?" Immediately our knowledge, wisdom, and awareness begin to shine. It's so beautiful and healthy. Many times the Buddha taught that one's own mindfulness is the best advisor or teacher. You don't have to call on anyone else from outside—you activate your own teacher. That is the best. Mindfulness is really so important. It will help us to continually advance on the path of our inner journey as we adventure through inner space to discover our enlightened qualities.

8. PERFECT CONCENTRATION

To review what we've discussed so far, we can divide the Noble Eightfold Path into three groups. (1) The first group includes perfect view and perfect understanding. (2) The second group is perfect speech, perfect activity, and perfect livelihood. (3) The third group is perfect effort, perfect mindfulness, and perfect concentration. We are on the last one—concentration, which deals directly with the mind.

Once we have beautiful mindfulness, the next noble path is perfect concentration. Concentration is mostly related to mind and meditation. Mind is everything. We speak according to our mind's instructions and we act according our mind's instructions. All our physical and verbal activities start from the mind. Whether we notice it immediately or not, it's true. That's what's happening. Our mind is always hovering and wandering, roaming and circling in the habitual world of mostly negative emotions. It's grasping, clinging, and discriminating. If we get more serious, our mind is constantly involved with the poisons: ignorance, attachment, anger, jealousy, hatred, doubt, hesitation, discouragement, and so forth. That's what's happening.

Our mind is running virtually 24 hours a day, except when we're in deep sleep. According to Buddhism, when we're in deep sleep our mind goes into a deeper level of consciousness, known as the *alaya*. Otherwise, mind is running all the time. During the day it's wandering in the brain with daytime phenomena, and at nighttime it's wandering in the dream world. It's wandering in the habitual world with habitual patterns, never really resting at all. Since birth, mind just keeps running. According to the Buddha's teaching, it's been running since beginningless time. Yet what does all this running actually accomplish? It disturbs the beauty of the inner nature of mind. It covers up our beauty with the dark pollution of habitual patterns, not letting it shine through. In the Buddha's teaching, concentration breaks up that pollution and gives the mind a rest. Concentration is meditation. It's relaxing. Therefore, it's good to meditate! As many of you already know, there are two different meditations: Shamatha meditation and Vipashyana meditation.

In Shamatha meditation, we're concentrating our mind. That means we're keeping our mind in a state of stillness. Since our mind is running all the time, now we're going to keep the mind still, and we do that by using effort. We put the mind in a state of stillness. For that period of time, the mind is not running or wandering. It's staying put. That's why it's called *shamatha*. Shamatha is a Sanskrit word that means "abiding in a state of calmness." We let the mind rest.

To begin this meditation, the great lineage masters always say to first bring up more joy and appreciation. As we've discussed, our life is so precious. Life is really so beautiful and special. Even though we all have difficulties sometimes, if we carefully count up the percentage out of a hundred, I think we can say that 80-85% of our life is good. That's a big percentage! If we gave 85% approval to politicians, they would all say, "Wow! You have a landslide victory!" And everyone would shake heads in agreement. To compare with 25%, 50%, or even 75%, 85% is a big majority! So since we already have a majority of goodness, gradually we can turn that into 100% good. We truly have the upper hand. If we have 75% or 85% good—definitely we can change 15%. 15% will not ruin our 85%. It's in our hands. Therefore bring more joy and appreciation. Joy and appreciation are enlightenment qualities. I always think of joy, appreciation, love, kindness, and compassion as similar to Jacob's ladder. They are the lights shining from our primordial nature through the dense clouds of habitual patterns. They are the light beams of our beautiful buddha-nature. In a way, they're shining out to rescue us. If we actively bring up all that light, joy and appreciation, love, kindness, and compassion, then our whole system will change. The whole world changes in that beautiful context.

So bring up more joy and appreciation, kindness, compassion, and bodhichitta thoughts for all sentient beings and then chant prayers. Prayer is the call of our devotion, the call of our love and compassion, the call of our deepest aspirations. This is wonderful! We have such a beautiful wish and intention. We want to become enlightened, just like the Buddha. We'd like to become a buddha ourselves. Prayer is the call to the buddhas, the call to all enlightened beings. It has nothing to do with a particular tradition or religion—we're calling to our own true nature. Make that call! If you don't know the prayers, then bring up joy and appreciation. Sincerely wish, "By the blessings of all the enlightened beings, may I actualize this beautiful samadhi of concentration, just as you buddhas and enlightened beings did." Strongly wish this, and then begin your meditation session and concentrate.

When it comes to concentration practice, you can begin with your breath. Don't change your breathing—just relax your body and your entire system. You're trying to keep everything in the natural state. Maintain the beautiful body postures if you know them. If not, just feel that everything is settled exactly in its own spot. Everything is balanced. Feel that your body is balanced, feel that all the channels of your nervous system are balanced, and feel that all of your wind energies are balanced. Now your mind is ready to return to balance and relax. Really feel that everything is balanced. Earth is balanced, space is balanced, and nature is balanced. See the balance of harmony and peace, and relax in this peaceful state.

With this thought, watch your breathing. You don't have to change your breathing—just keep it exactly normal. Let it come in and out of your nostrils. The breath is coming in and out . . . simply follow your breathing. As it goes in, let your thought follow your breathing. When you inhale, be aware that breath is coming in. As you exhale, be aware of the breath going out. See that. This is called mindfulness. Mindfulness is keeping you beautifully relaxed as you breathe. Just keep that circle of breaths, in and out, in and out. If you'd like, you can count the breaths as one, two, three, four, all the way up to five or ten. Then start again at one. In is one, and out is two. Or you can count one inhalation and exhalation together as one. However you want to count is up to you, but keep your mind with the breathing, or with the number if you're counting the breaths. The mind doesn't go outside this. We're putting the mind in some degree of a gentle passage so it doesn't become irregular.

Relax. This is training the mind. We're training our mind so it can rest and relax, and then we can discover the beauty of our mind. Practice this for five or ten minutes, or for however long you can according to your time and capability. Regardless of how long you meditate, or which object of concentration you choose, try and maintain really good concentration. Sometimes if you'd like you can also concentrate on a small object right in front of you. Just concentrate and look to that object. Your mind is with your eyes, and your eyes are with that object. Mind, eye, and object come into one single state. See how long you can concentrate. Just try it and see. See if you can stay with that concentration for one minute or half a minute. Eventually your mind will move. It will get restless and go away. But as soon as you notice, immediately bring your mind back into focus in the same manner, without complaining or getting tired and bored. Just keep doing that again and again. If we keep our concentration with joy and mindfulness, that is known as the noble path of perfect concentration.

CHAPTER 7

ETHICS: THE FOUNDATION OF THE SPIRITUAL PATH

Four Friends Working Together

In general, all the teachings of the Buddha can be summarized into three categories, known as the Three Baskets: (1) *Vinaya* teachings, (2) *Sutra* teachings, and (3) *Abhidharma* teachings. The principle meaning of all the Vinaya teachings is morality, or ethics; the principle meaning of the Sutras is concentration; and the principle meaning of the Abhidharma is wisdom, or teachings on the true nature of great emptiness. These Three Basket teachings go from gross, to subtle, and very subtle states of mind.

The Vinaya teachings emphasize bringing the outer level actions of body, speech, and mind into a gentler, more peaceful, soothing, and calm state. That is really the principal teaching of the Vinaya. In the *Mahayanasutralankara*, or the *Ornament of the Mahayana Sutras*, the Future Buddha Maitreya and great master Asanga said that when practitioners really train in the Vinaya, their body, speech, and mind become so gentle. They are calm and feel more contentment. In general, this is the essence of the Vinaya teachings.

The great master Longchenpa, along with many other masters, summarized the teachings of the Vinaya as avoiding harmful actions. Avoid any action that is harmful to yourself and others, either directly or indirectly. That is the essence of the Vinaya teachings. When we we're able to practice this, it makes our body, speech, and mind very calm, peaceful, and gentle. Many times the teachings say that when people have really beautiful discipline and morality, they are very soothing, calming, and nice. If you look at them from far away, you can tell that they have some kind of special quality, even if they aren't really doing anything.

There's a true story in the Buddha's Vinaya teaching about a man in Shravasti named Nesu Tamdzin Tilap who had seven daughters. He didn't have any sons, and was quite poor. Luckily, all seven of his daughters married, but they too were quite poor. His wife was a talker—she talked all the time, and was always talking kind of sharply. One day, all seven daughters came home to visit and brought their husbands, but there wasn't enough food for everyone. The seven daughters were all talking so much— just talk, talk, talk—and the old man was responsible for making everyone calm and peaceful, but he was so tired and felt so bored. He thought it was just like burning in a fire in his house. There was no rest. Then the time came that he had to plow his field. He had one small piece of land to plow, but he didn't have two oxen. He only had one, so he needed to borrow another one. He went to a family friend to borrow an ox, and then plowed for one full day and felt so tired. He thought, "When I plow the field, I have to walk so much and work so hard, and then I go home and don't have any peace." Of course he was poor, and all his daughters and relatives were there needing something from him, so he was really thinking what to do. The next day he thought to go and plow, but unfortunately the ox that he borrowed was somehow lost. It was gone. Now he was in big trouble. What to do? He felt so sad and lost, sitting on his farmland with no hope.

He was so upset thinking of all these things, but then far in the distance, he saw a monk meditating under a tree. When he saw the monk, he thought, "Wow, that's such a beautiful, calm person. How lucky he is." Gazing at him, he thought, "I should go and talk with him. He looks so gentle—maybe it will make me more calm and peaceful." So he went to him and said, "You look so calm. You look so peaceful and soothing. You look so great!" He really said that. And then the monk said, "Yes, that's true. I am calm, I am peaceful, and I am really in a very good state." Of course, displaying these beautiful qualities has merit—having good morality really brings more calm and peace. We're using mindfulness, alertness, and conscientiousness to reduce our wild habitual patterns. These three really help us remain balanced.

Bodhichitta, refuge, and morality are the ground of all the practices taught by the Buddha. Morality is the ground. Without morality and ethics, spirituality is lost. This is not only true on the spiritual level, but without morality the valuable worldly aspects of samsara are also lost. Therefore, morality is the ground. Refuge is the ground and bodhichitta is the ground. With a solid ground we're no longer hovering in the sky—we're beautifully grounded. We aren't jiggling or twisting around. We aren't shaking like rattlesnakes. We're grounded like a mountain, standing firm and tall and beautiful. That's what we have with good morality. Our great master Khenchen Palden Sherab Rinpoche often quoted Nagarjuna, who said, "If you have morality—even the samsara level of ethics—you aren't far from the Dharma, or from heaven." With the firm ground of morality, every good thing can grow.

CHAPTER 8

DISTINGUISHING BENEFICIAL ACTIONS FROM HARMFUL ACTIONS

Victorious Creatures of Harmony:
Natural Enemies Resolving Their Differences

Let's examine morality and discipline in greater detail from the perspective of the ten non-virtuous actions. As we briefly discussed in Chapter 6, of the ten non-virtuous actions, three are related to body, four to speech, and three to mind.

1. Killing
2. Stealing
3. Sexual misconduct

4. Deceiving speech
5. Slander
6. Harsh speech
7. Gossip

8. Covetousness
9. Malice
10. Wrong view

The three non-virtuous actions related to body are: (1) taking life, (2) taking the possessions of others without permission, or stealing, and (3) sexual misconduct. Regarding the first, taking life, Buddhism teaches that all of life is precious, and that each and every sentient being has an important purpose in the universe, even if we can't see it. We must not disrupt this. Furthermore, when we take a life, we shorten our own lifespan—not only for this lifetime, but in future lifetimes as well. This is due to the law of cause and effect, or karma. Even to unintentionally take the life of another being is bad; so too is wishing to take a life. The worst situation is when we wish to kill, do the killing, and celebrate the deed. Negative emotions always accompany the taking of life. For example, there's anger when we destroy an enemy; greed when we murder someone in order to steal; desire when we slay an animal to eat its flesh; ignorance when soldiers kill for their country and when people kill for religious reasons. It's so important that we do not kill. Rather, we should recognize and appreciate the value of life and pray for the longevity of all beings.

The second non-virtuous action related to body is stealing. Stealing can be done through power, stealth, and fraud. Stealing through power is when people with political, social, or physical authority simply take what doesn't belong to them. Stealing through stealth is robbery done in secrecy or by surprise. Stealing through fraud includes all kinds of deceptive business schemes and practices. When we take another's possessions without permission, the gains are illusory. The real result will be intense mental and material impoverishment in this and future lifetimes. We must understand that each person has his or her own portion, or share of wealth because of past karma. We should be satisfied with what we have, and not look with envy upon those who are wealthier than us. Instead, we should be happy for them, and rejoice in their good merit.

The third non-virtuous action of the body is sexual misconduct. Sexual misconduct can be characterized as either worldly or related to the Dharma. Worldly sexual misconduct includes having relations with someone else's husband or wife, or with a prostitute. It also includes relations that violate society's laws and rape. Sexual misconduct according to the Dharma always involves breaking the vows you promised to keep.

Next are the four categories of non-virtuous speech: (1) deceit, (2) slander, (3) harsh words, and (4) gossip. Deceitful speech can be further divided into three: ordinary, arrogant, and extraordinary. We practice ordinary deceitful speech in order to gain temporary benefit from others, like when we represent ourselves as being better or higher than we are, or when we make promises we can't keep. Arrogant deceitful speech is when we try to convince someone of something we don't know, like a charlatan healer or fortune-teller. Extraordinary deceitful speech means we represent ourselves as having great mystical abilities by pretending to be a great master or an enlightened being to win prestige, power, or wealth.

Slanderous speech can be direct or indirect. Indirect slanderous speech occurs when we speak falsely about someone who isn't physically present. Direct slander occurs when we do it right in front of someone. In both cases, slander is used to hurt the person's reputation. Slander is particularly bad when it occurs within a Sangha, whether it's between students or between a student and teacher.

There are three types of harsh speech. One is openly criticizing someone who is actually present. Even if this is done calmly, if the intent is negative, it's still considered harsh speech. The second is speaking out of anger and demeaning someone. It doesn't matter if what's said is true—it's still harsh speech. This includes all kinds of name-calling and cursing. The third kind of harsh speech is called "covert." This is any kind of negative speech that pretends to be positive.

Gossip means to talk idly about others. Even if there's no apparent motive to cause harm, gossip stimulates both negative emotions and an overly critical mindset, in the moment and also in the future.

Regarding the mind, the three non-virtuous actions are (1) covetousness, (2) malice, and (3) wrong views. Covetousness means to long with envy for something another person has. Malice is thinking ill of others, wishing them harm or misfortune. Wrong views include ignoring and flaunting the laws of cause and effect by holding extreme positions like eternalism, nihilism, and overblown self-centeredness.

The ten non-virtuous actions arise from the six poisons, either singly or in combinations. The first of the six poisons—the root of them all—is ignorance. Out of ignorance comes desire, anger, pride, jealousy, and doubt. Non-virtuous actions motivated mainly by ignorance will lead us to be reborn in the animal realms; by desire, to the realm of the hungry ghosts; by anger, to the hell realms; by pride, to the god realms; by jealousy, to the realm of the anti-gods; and by doubt, to the human realm. These six realms are known as the *bardo*, or "intermediate state."

The bardo is experienced during this lifetime, the space between lives, and in future lifetimes. Essentially, the bardo is the interval from the beginning of delusion until we return to our primordial nature. All our wandering in between is the bardo. Until we reach enlightenment, everything we feel, know, and experience, is bardo phenomena. Even now, we're wandering in an intermediate state. This will continue as long as we persist in clinging to the dualistic belief in the inherent existence of self and world.

In order to wake up from mistaken bardo experiences, and to stop creating the causes for our own suffering, we have to avoid the ten non-virtuous actions and perform their opposites—the *ten virtuous actions*. These are (1) respecting, protecting, and nurturing the lives of others, (2) sharing and giving to others, (3) respecting our vows and commitments regarding sexual activity, (4) speaking the truth, (5) speaking to make peace, (6) speaking kindly, (7) speaking meaningfully, (8) being content, (9) cultivating love and compassion, and (10) cultivating an open and relaxed mind, and practicing Dharma.

CHAPTER 9

SHARPEN YOUR WISDOM WITH THE THREE TRAININGS

Sword of Wisdom

All of the Buddha's teachings are summarized into three types of extraordinary trainings: (1) gentleness or ethical conduct, (2) concentration, and (3) wisdom. These are known as *tsultrim* [*tshul khrims*], *samten* [*bsamg tan*], and *sherab* [*shes rab*] in Tibetan, and *shila*, *samadhi*, and *prajna* in Sanskrit. All of the various practices taught by the Buddha are included in these three types of training. Each has a very special result and a specific benefit.

Training in gentleness is also known as discipline or morality. Discipline, morality, and gentleness are very closely related, and are all included in this type of training. This training brings gentleness into all of our activities and helps to overcome the wild, scattered activities of body, speech, and mind. The results of this training mainly affect our body and speech. Our outward activities and speech become more gentle, which makes it is possible to understand each other in ways that are more harmonious and peaceful.

The second training of concentration deals more directly with the mind. Concentration is a method used to overcome the way the mind is scattered and unfocused. It brings the mind to a single sharp point of awareness and holds it there. The result is similar to the first training in that it brings more gentleness by developing a calm and clear mental state.

The third training of wisdom transcends moral discipline and concentration, and brings a perfect understanding of samsara and nirvana. It is the final and ultimate training that transforms the whole system of our body, speech, and mind into a new understanding, even a new reality. Mipham Rinpoche refers to it as the "perfect view of the true nature." This true nature isn't located externally—it can only be found in the mind.

Training in wisdom involves finding the exact facts about reality. These facts lead to the realization that everything exists only in this moment. They also demonstrate that all things are impermanent and interdependent, working together in an interconnected network of causes and effects. All phenomena, even the self, are based on many, many things. Nothing exists independently in an unchanging state. Instead, there are hundreds of millions of interacting parts and pieces working together to create the experience of any moment.

The underlying "oneness" of all things must be understood in the context that each thing has many parts working together that create a phenomena that we label with a name and consider a separate entity in the world. This illustrates the composite nature of things. This is called "clear" or "perfect understanding."

Training in wisdom has two main parts: first is realizing that everything is changing, and second, that things exist only in the moment. These two parts can be realized through self-examination. For example, from birth until now our bodies are constantly changing. Seasons continuously change, and everyday we experience the cycle of day and night. Everything is constantly changing.

When we don't accept change, we suffer. Clinging and grasping onto things only increases our attachment, and when things change—as they inevitably do—it causes suffering. When we closely examine where suffering comes from, it becomes apparent that suffering doesn't exist externally. Suffering is an internal, subjective state of emotional and mental awareness. Suffering is connected to the physical as well as to the mental. Of course it's obviously related to the body, but upon detailed examination we realize that the deeper experience of suffering is in the mind. All emotions and feelings ultimately depend on the mind. Emotional experiences are part of the mind, experienced within the mind.

Still, if suffering is a mental event, is it possible to determine exactly where it exists in the mind? Suffering itself has no material existence. Yet trying to locate suffering in the mind quickly reveals that the mind itself has no solid material existence. The Buddha's Abhidharma teachings state that there are fifty-one types of mental events, and it lists suffering as one of them.

Regarding the cause of suffering, careful examination reveals that the cause of suffering is related to clinging and attachment, and that the root cause is clinging to the idea of "self." The root of emotional reactivity—both positive and negative—is ego-clinging.

To apply this analytical meditation to ego-clinging, begin by examining exactly where ego-clinging is located, and look for its cause. We usually think the ego is located somewhere within the body. But upon further examination, there's no exact location of the ego—it obviously has no material or physical existence on its own. The ego is a function of the mind. It's part of the way that the mind thinks and reacts.

Our investigation then leads us to how did the ego begin, or what caused the ego? A careful examination shows that it's made up of many physical and mental components, and each of these has its own distinct causes and conditions. After all these parts come together to form the ego, that's when it has its own continuity. With these conditions in place, the sense of self, "I," or ego is formed.

Look at your ego and investigate it using the wisdom aspect of mental training. Follow the logical progression of the analysis. Upon investigation, the ego cannot be found as a material object, nor can the location of its existence be found. The ego cannot be found apart from the body. The more it's investigated, the more it becomes apparent that there is actually nothing to find.

The ego, just like everything else, is based in great emptiness. On the relative level, the ego is very clearly experienced. But upon investigation using this wisdom technique, we clearly see that the ego has no existence at all on the ultimate level. It only exists on the phenomenal level as a mental event—it's just an idea, a mere conception. The ego is composed of numerous things that are temporarily combined, working together in a system of interdependent coordination.

Everything continually moves from moment to moment, and each moment things are in a state of change. This realization transcends duality, going beyond the limitations of the ego to the understanding of the true nature of great emptiness. In the Dzogchen teachings, this is called the "view." Maintaining your mind in this awareness is simply relaxing into the natural view of reality. Without this realization, the ego is continually caught in duality, which gets very tiring and boring. This analytic meditation shows how the mind continually moves from this realization of emptiness back into the attitude of ego-clinging. There are many very powerful habitual tendencies that continually bring our minds back to the regular, mundane way of looking at the world.

The moment you realize that your mind has gone back to regular ego-clinging, it's very important to catch the mind and return to the larger, more expansive view of reality. The more your mind can be in the view of great emptiness, the more it will soften all the negative emotions of ignorance, attachment, and anger. Very naturally, they will no longer be experienced in the same way that we experience them when we're grasping to ego.

Until we can maintain this wisdom all the time, it's necessary to meditate using the analytic wheel of investigation. This technique increasingly deepens our realization that everything is compounded and exists only in the momentary state of its appearance. Using this wheel of analytic meditation develops the wisdom awareness to overcome all ego-clinging, and over time, our realization of the transparent state of all phenomena will become more stable.

Our goal is to transcend thoughts rather than habitually pursue them. When you're new to the path, it's very important to spend time analyzing and investigating physical and mental objects very thoroughly. As your understanding becomes clearer, you naturally decrease the frequency and intensity of this type of analysis and investigation. As your certainty wisdom increases, your doubts and hesitation lessen. At that point, it becomes possible to meditate without clinging and running after every concept and topic that arises in your mind.

The analytic meditation practice combines joyful effort with an understanding of various states of mind. The mind is refreshed by abiding in meditation within the bounds of your understanding. By applying mindfulness, you learn that it's possible to notice the very instant that bad habits, emotions, or any form of grasping or clinging arises. With awareness, there's no opportunity for these habits to occupy your mind since you become aware of them the very instant they appear. This type of awareness immediately transcends and liberates habits into the wisdom of the true nature.

In general, if mindfulness and alertness are applied the very moment that negative emotions arise, they serve as an antidote to those emotions, and the resultant negativity immediately stops. Applying mindfulness instantly causes you to regain the original state where negativities naturally dissolve. They automatically disappear. It's similar to when the sun rises in the east—darkness simultaneously disappears in the sunlight. A clear understanding of the system of the mind reveals the reality of samsara and nirvana within the natural state of mind.

The Three Trainings of morality, concentration, and wisdom

support one another to increasingly sharpen your discriminating wisdom to analyze both external and internal phenomena in a way that is free from exaggerating or diminishing reality as it is. These teachings are about discovering the true nature—the exact reality of everything, internally and externally.

CHAPTER 10

STAYING ON TRACK WITH MINDFULNESS

Ven. Khenchen Palden Sherab Rinpoche

Before we receive any teachings or begin any practice, it's always important to cultivate mindfulness. Mindfulness is important all the time—not just at certain times or for particular practices. Whether we're starting a practice, contemplating, or meditating, we need to be mindful. Even when we receive teachings and are familiar with the subject of the teachings, we should continually maintain our mindfulness so that the strength and energy of the teachings we receive doesn't become spoiled and disappear. Mindfulness is important because it makes our practice whole. It keeps the practice very active, beautiful, and on target. Cultivating mindfulness is especially important when we're just starting out on the path, but the bottom line is that, for every practitioner, the development of one's practice depends on mindfulness.

Of course, the topic of mindfulness isn't new. We're all familiar with how important it is. When we're mindful, everything falls beautifully into place. Whether we're involved in worldly or spiritual activities, we need to develop mindfulness. When we possess mindfulness, we're always alert and careful. Thus, the nature of mindfulness is intelligence, wisdom, consideration, understanding, and knowledge. It's what makes our selves and our activities beautiful, bringing the various Dharma teachings together perfectly.

Mindfulness prevents us from performing all kinds of ignorant, negative, and improper activities that aren't good for us or other beings. It reduces negative actions and brings the strength of wisdom, joy, and appreciation. Everything becomes clear. Having mindfulness, we shine a beautiful spotlight on ourselves and polish our knowledge and wisdom, which, as a result, will no longer be able to hide in a corner, in the bushes, or anywhere else.

Buddha Shakyamuni taught that every one of his teachings and all of our commitments must be rooted in mindfulness. In his teachings on proper conduct, which are collectively known as the Vinaya, the Glorious Conqueror concluded each of his discourses on rules and guidelines with a teaching on mindfulness. The Buddha also talked about mindfulness in the bodhisattva path, which includes all the guidelines for bodhisattvas—such as those related with loving-kindness, compassion, and wisdom—and the many Vajrayana teachings. Therefore, mindfulness is something we always need. It's important because it makes everything beautiful, harmonious, and peaceful. Mindfulness makes all the wonderful qualities we honor and appreciate immediately available, more in the spotlight, and easier to use at all times. As a result, we all feel very happy when we have mindfulness.

In his *Guide to the Bodhisattva's Way of Life*, the great master Shantideva said that if we don't have mindfulness, our knowledge will seep away like excellent food or liquid in a leaky bowl. Even if we feel good about how wonderful something is, if we don't sustain it with mindfulness, it won't really benefit us in the long run. Then we end up forgetting how to use it when we want to. It's almost like losing something very special, even though it may have been something previously appreciated and viewed as beautiful. Therefore, particularly during meditation, whether we're doing Shamatha or Vipashyana meditation, mindfulness is important because it will refresh the energy and strength of our practice, learning, and knowledge.

One of the first teachings given by Buddha Shakyamuni was on the four different kinds of mindfulness. They are (1) mindfulness of body, (2) mindfulness of sensations, (3) mindfulness of mind, and (4) mindfulness of phenomena. The nature of mindfulness is intelligence. Joyful effort, courage, commitment, joy, and appreciation come naturally when we have mindfulness. In this regard, the Buddha's teachings often explain that the correct state of mindfulness is wisdom. Thus, mindfulness is that which is regarded by the mind with intelligence or wisdom.

MINDFULNESS OF BODY

Mindfulness of the body is reflected in our physical being. We all know our bodies are very precious, important, and spacious. But we also know that our bodies have many different parts. The body isn't only made up of one specific object: it's complex, like a mechanical object with various parts all joined together. When we start thinking about all the components that work together in order to make this beautiful human body, we begin to see that each part is further composed of many different particles and systems, and all of these complex systems and parts come together to make this beautiful body. Hence the human body isn't just one independently existing, solid form; rather, it's a whole integral system. For this reason, the Vajrayana teachings often say the human body is a universe. It's complex, like life itself. The body is in an active state continually reflecting all the systems and parts included within it. It also contains all the different elements of fire, wind, water, earth, and space.

The human body is beautiful, and each and every one is very precious. And yet it's a magical illusion! When we examine it from a deeper and more precise level, we find that the form of the body is neither substantial nor solid. We can further appreciate the functioning of the beautiful human body by first reflecting on it at the gross level, then more subtle levels, and then contemplating our habitual patterns of grasping and clinging. What we have now is so very special. We should feel joy and appreciation, taking full advantage of this precious human life by doing good things for ourselves and others. Also, by thinking of the human body on a subtler and more detailed level, we can see that it's composed of atomic particles that are neither substantial nor solidly existing. Based on our investigation, we can then appreciate and use the body well, relaxing and meditating without grasping or clinging to it. This is basically known as practicing mindfulness of the body.

MINDFULNESS OF SENSATIONS

The second mindfulness is that of sensations or physical feelings, which is a more subtle investigation than mindfulness of the body. Obviously, physical sensations are important to every single one of us. They can be divided into three types: (1) feelings of pleasure, (2) feelings of displeasure, and (3) neutral feelings. But what are these feelings, really? By thoroughly examining feelings that arise on the physical and mental levels, we discover that they don't exist in a substantial or solid way. When feelings of pleasure or displeasure arise at the physical or mental level, we must ask ourselves where they come from. Again, when we try to locate and examine them, we find that they're activated by a complex combination of mental impressions and physical sensations that aren't substantial, solid, or independently existent. Understanding this and then relaxing in the natural state of mind without grasping or clinging is known as mindfulness meditation on physical sensations.

MINDFULNESS OF MIND

The third mindfulness is that of the mind itself. According to the Buddha's teachings, there are two different aspects of mind, known as "principal mind" and "mental events." Principal mind is consciousness, which can actually be divided into eight different consciousnesses. The eight consciousnesses include the five sense consciousnesses of (1) sight, (2) sound, (3) smell, (4) taste, and (5) touch, the (6) sixth consciousness of dualistic mind, the (7) seventh afflictive-emotion consciousness, and the (8) eighth consciousness of the all-ground storehouse, or alaya. All the various mental events can be divided into fifty-one different mental states.

Principal mind and all mental events are neither independent nor solidly existing. They're categorized in terms of what they reflect in the mind, how they function, and what they communicate. Therefore, whether we speak of principal mind or mental events, both are aspects of the mind. So these divisions all reflect different displays of mind, categorized into different types of mind. Again, there's no substantial, solidly existing mind. If we follow and break down each aspect of a mental event, we see that there's really nothing to find. As in the Dzogchen teachings, we must look for where a thought comes from, where it goes, and where it resides, ultimately recognizing the insubstantiality and lack of solidity of each thought. Having this clear image and understanding of the mind's natural state—and relaxing in that state—is known as mindfulness meditation on the mind itself.

MINDFULNESS OF PHENOMENA

The fourth mindfulness, known as mindfulness of phenomena, doesn't simply involve focusing on the body, sensations, or mind. In this case, our focus is the entire universe, whether it's mind, body, feelings, subject, or object. Mindfulness of phenomena increases our knowledge of all existing phenomena.

Phenomena can be divided into two categories: "compounded phenomena" and "uncompounded phenomena." Compounded phenomena can be further subdivided into the five aggregates of (1) form, (2) feelings, (3) perceptions, (4) mental formations, and (5) consciousness, which are composed of the fire, water, wind, and earth elements, and supported by the element of space. Uncompounded phenomena include the two types of cessation—liberation from samsara and complete enlightenment—and space.

Whether phenomena are compounded or uncompounded, the Buddhadharma considers them part of phenomenal existence; everything is included within phenomenal existence. For this reason, when we think about phenomena—existent or nonexistent, compounded or uncompounded—upon examination, we find that they don't possess a substantial or solid existence. The same can be said of the body, physical sensations, and mind: all are in a continual process of change. They're all interdependent, functioning precisely according to the system of the twelve links of dependent origination. The nature of interdependence is reflected in all phenomena, therefore no single phenomenon arises outside the process of dependent origination. Everything we see, think, or feel has many direct and indirect ingredients and interacting parts that operate both on the gross level and behind the scenes of our experience. In other words, nothing happens independently of its own accord. This is the nature of all phenomena, both subjects and objects. Knowing this clearly and exactly as it is while relaxing the mind in its natural state is basically mindfulness meditation on phenomena. This process is also described in the Dzogchen teachings.

To have mindfulness means we bring our knowledge of every single thing, including knowledge of our body, feelings, mind, and all phenomena into the spotlight. In this context, relaxing ourselves in the natural state of mind is known simply as mindfulness practice. Mindfulness encompasses both wisdom and intelligence, which means we're not just going to leap at things hidden in the corner. Rather, we're going to look at our own experience and be more active, beneficial, and effective for the benefit of ourselves and others. It's mindfulness that allows us to achieve this aim.

Everything moves forward when we have mindfulness.

The opposite of mindfulness is forgetfulness and dullness, as well as neglecting, ignoring, and missing out on many things. Without mindfulness, our goals, aims, targets, and destinations are spoiled; our nature, identity, foundation, and philosophy are quickly blown away. The result is all kinds of sloppy things like forgetfulness, fogginess, ignorance, dullness, and laziness. Each of these obscurations undermine us both directly and indirectly, dragging us down into the ditch of habitual patterns and carrying us away. Therefore, mindfulness is very special and beautiful, something we always need.

The Inner Tantra teachings of the Buddha also emphasize mindfulness, explaining that we always need to turn the spinning wheel of mindfulness without distraction. We don't become distracted when we have mindfulness. As a result, we must be mindful during our Dzogchen meditation. If we don't have mindfulness, various scattered, foggy, and discursive thoughts will undermine our brilliant awareness of the present. For all these reasons, we need mindfulness when we do the foundation practices, as well as during our Dzogchen meditation practice. It's also important to engage in any meditation postures and gestures with mindfulness.

Mindfulness is our greatest support. It will put us on the right track. And once we're on track, mindfulness helps us continue with perfect balance. Then our journey to enlightenment will be smooth and beautiful. Additionally, when we've developed more stable mindfulness, every moment of our life can be guided by it. In this world, not only will our Dharma practice of mindfulness make us very beautiful—it will safely usher us towards our final moment on earth. Then, even during the last moments of our lives, mindfulness will lead us beautifully on to the next stage in the bardo after death. That's why great Dzogchen masters leave this world with immense joy: they're joyous because their mindfulness provides the brilliant clarity, luminosity, and light that brightens the passageways of their journey.

The Inner Tantras say that if we don't reach enlightenment within this lifetime, there will be excellent opportunities to reach enlightenment or higher realization at the moment of death. That final push and breakthrough takes place with mindfulness. If somehow we also miss that opportunity, the Dzogchen teachings state that after we pass away, there will be other great opportunities to reach higher, more stable states of realization or even enlightenment. If we maintain stable mindfulness, it will ignite our realization so we can connect with the true nature of our mind. If somehow we miss these opportunities, other additional opportunities for realization will arise in the bardo after death, and at the very least, we can positively influence our next birth to continue our Dharma practice.

CHAPTER 11

HOW TO MEDITATE

Ven. Khenpo Tsewang Dongyal Rinpoche

When we come to the practice of meditation, there are two techniques that we have to apply: Calm Abiding and Insight, which are known as Shamatha and Vipashyana in Sanskrit.

Naturally, there are different types of practitioners. For some practitioners it's good to practice these separately at first. Eventually our goal is for Shamatha and Vipashyana to become a union, not separate. That's the goal, but to first jumpstart our practice according to our capabilities, some people prefer to start with Shamatha, and then later focus more on Vipashyana. Then when they come to Vipashyana, they gradually combine the two so they become a union.

On the other hand, some practitioners start with both Shamatha and Vipashyana immediately without any separation or without going through different stages. It depends on the individual which approach is more beneficial or suitable. In reality, Shamatha and Vipashyana aren't different—they're both the same and are both naturally in union.

CALM ABIDING MEDITATION

The Sanskrit word *shamatha* is made of two words: *shama* and *tha*. *Shama* means "peaceful" or "calm," and *tha* means "letting" or "abiding," so Shamatha means "letting the mind be peaceful." Shamatha is also known in Sanskrit as *samadhi*. *Sama* means "motionless" and *dhi* means "holding," so samadhi means maintaining one's mind in a constant, unchanging state. For example, if you fill a bowl with water and don't touch it, the water doesn't move. It stays still. Similarly, when your mind rests single-pointedly, undisturbed by thoughts, it becomes calm.

Calm Abiding is a type of meditation where you train the mind to not be disturbed by any other thoughts—you choose what to concentrate on, and you stay with that concentration. There are many different techniques or approaches to Shamatha, but what is it exactly? Shamatha means stopping conceptions, or stopping our wild, scattered thoughts. You're going to block thoughts, or stop them from constantly moving all the time.

When we meditate, we have to relax our mind. We shouldn't follow after any thoughts. We have to stay wherever we concentrate our mind. At the present moment our minds are blowing in the wind, constantly moving forward. With Shamatha meditation, we're putting a brake on that moving wind so it stays wherever we place our concentration. We're training to have our mind remain exactly where we want it to stay.

In the *Lamp of Mahamudra*, the great master Tsele Natsok Rangdrol says to start Shamatha practice by first trying to reduce your gross level thoughts to more subtle thoughts. In order to reduce gross level thoughts using this particular technique, you don't just block the thoughts forcefully. Instead you're going to use techniques that utilize your intelligence. As a thought arises, look directly at it and think: (1) Where is this thought coming from? (2) Where is the thought going? (3) Where is the thought right now? Really try to see the answer clearly. When you use these three investigations, you won't actually be able to find any thoughts. Then just stay there and don't make any further inquiry. Try to just remain in that state of non-thought.

The great master says that relaxing in that no-thought state after these three investigations is similar to a Zen "*koan.*" When we investigate this koan—where is this thought coming from, where is it going, and where is it now—we realize that we're not going to find an answer, so we begin to settle our minds in the natural state of empty openness. This empty openness isn't only the no-thought state of Shamatha—it's also very close to Vipashyana. It's based on Shamatha, but it also brings the energy or quality of Vipashyana right there. Therefore, this is a very, very powerful and special technique that ushers you from the duality world of conceptions to the state of non-conception, free from duality.

When we're relaxing our minds in that state of openness, calmly abiding with those techniques, most of the time we can't stay relaxed for very long. Immediately, or after a few seconds, thoughts will come up. Yet whenever a thought comes—whether it takes a few seconds, minutes, or however long—let it come, but don't follow after it. Instead of going after it and chasing it, look back toward the thought with your mind.

As a result of this meditation, three different experiences will come up. The first experience is known as a stream rushing down a mountain. The second experience is known as a smooth running river, and the third experience is an unmoving ocean.

For beginning meditators, the first experience is like a stream rushing down the side of a mountain. We all know how fast and strong streams rush down from mountains. Similarly, when meditators first begin to meditate, the mind becomes even busier—even more unstable and restless than during normal, ordinary times. That's the first experience. The Dzogchen teachings often mention that our minds have always been like that, but we just didn't recognize it. Now with meditation, we're putting the movement of our minds in a radar spotlight and so we're noticing it more, but our minds have always been like this, or maybe even busier.

Now we're beginning to notice, which means our minds are slowing down under the radar spotlight of our awareness. So that is the first good experience.

If we continue having these experiences, we shouldn't see them as mistakes and become discouraged by the movements of mind. Instead we should restrengthen our meditation and bring up more joy and devotion, and inspire ourselves to do more meditation. We should continue to meditate as we've been doing, but even more strongly. Then as time goes on, if we continually do that, then as all the great, experienced practitioners and masters often say, the mind will become more calm and peaceful, and we'll begin to notice our thoughts slowing down. At that point, we'll almost be able to discipline our own minds by ourselves. The mind becomes more slowed down and calm, and at the same time, some degree of joy, peace, and happiness also arises in our minds. This peaceful state of the mind comes very naturally. These are all signs that your awareness is more stable. When this happens, it is the second experience of a slowing down, smooth river. Even though big rivers still move very strongly and steadily, there isn't as much turbulence going on. Compared to water gushing down a mountain, rivers are very smooth.

If we continue to meditate and practice, then that smooth river will eventually merge with the ocean. When we reach that state, our mind will become very calm and peaceful. There will hardly be any movement. At that point, when you begin to meditate your mind will stay so calm and peaceful...so relaxed, just like the ocean. At the same time, joy, peace, and happiness will all naturally arise so beautifully and nicely. Your body and mind will be more relaxed, in a blissful state. At the same time, there won't be too many gross conceptions or emotions disturbing you. And even if there are certain things going on around you, they won't affect you too much. This level of practitioner is able to continually maintain a calm, peaceful atmosphere both inwardly in their mind, as well as outwardly.

Different stages of certainty wisdom will also begin to shine as you go through these experiences, which are known as states of "omniscience." Your wisdom and realization are developing to some degree, and at the same time, you remain very calm, peaceful, easygoing, more down-to-earth, and in a very settled state. That's why the example used for this degree of mental stabilization is the calm, ocean-like, peaceful experience.

When you reach this third experience of meditation, you feel calm and peaceful, and everything is really nice. If we reach this stage, then we should always be watchful that this experience doesn't become a hindrance to the further development of our realization. The great master Tsele Natsok Rangdrol says that many times when meditators reach this stage it can slow down their development because they think they've already reached a very high realization. They're at quite a good stage, and at the same time other people are appreciating and respecting them more. Because of this, they feel quite good inside and might even think, "I'm really good now. I'm an accomplished practitioner. I've become a siddha." They get distracted by those kinds of attitudes and thoughts, and then progress in their meditation slows down. They may even get so carried away by the external appreciation and respect that they completely spoil their meditation. Here Tsele Natsok Rangdrol says that they're not just spoiling it for themselves, they can also spoil it for others too. Therefore, at this stage you must continue to restrengthen your meditation practice, contact a qualified teacher, correct and refine your realization, and then continually move forward.

To summarize, when we start doing Shamatha meditation, at the beginning there are three processes that naturally come. The first stage is like gushing, running water from a mountain range, which means that an experience of great restlessness comes. This isn't bad—we're just beginning to notice our restless mind. When that happens, continue your practice with all the beautiful attitudes that we discussed, full of joy and devotion. Continue to relax and stay with your meditation. When you continue in this way, the second experience comes, which is like a river moving across a meadow, or lower down on the ground in a plateau. It's still running, but it's softer and smoother than the gushing river. Again, continue your Shamatha meditation with a beautiful attitude of love and devotion. Next, the third experience will come which is like a river merging into the ocean. Now the mind becomes very settled. Even though some waves and tides occasionally appear, basically it's very settled.

INSIGHT MEDITATION

Once our minds are stable like the ocean, then we can begin to practice Vipashyana, or insight meditation. Vipashyana goes further than maintaining a calm and unmoving mind—in Vipashyana practice you examine the mind and its source. By penetrating the surface level of thoughts and emotions, you see that their insubstantiality is the true nature of mind.

Rather than focusing outside, Vipashyana meditation starts directly with the mind, beholding the true nature of the mind exactly as it is. Of course, there are many ways to do this, and eventually we also have to see objects in that same state, but we can't start there. We have to first begin with our own minds. This is also true in Dzogchen meditation—we start by recognizing the nature of our mind, or *rigpa*. We're beholding the innate nature of the mind, exactly as it is.

Vipashyana is a Sanskrit word made up of *vi*, which means "extraordinary," and *pashyana,* which means "seeing." Many times it's translated into English as "insight." However, if we translate it literally into English, it is "supreme seeing." This "seeing" is more special or superior to Shamatha; therefore it's supreme. You're seeing the nature *exactly* as it is—not through deduction or presumption. It's no longer theory now. You're directly experiencing the nature of the mind the very moment you look. That's why it's called "supreme seeing," "insight," or Vipashyana.

What is it that you see? You're seeing the true nature of mind exactly as it is. The nature of mind is free from every distinction and all conceptual categories. It doesn't exist or not exist, or both exist and not exist, or neither exist or not exist. It's beyond any possible way we try to conceptually understand it. In other words, it is beyond the grasping of duality mind. That is the nature of mind you're now beholding. We begin Vipashyana meditation by seeing the true nature of our mind, and then later on we include seeing the true nature of outer objects as well, and eventually the whole universe.

When we look to the mind, we see that the mind is clear and empty, yet there is no separation. We can't put the clarity aspect of the mind on one side and the empty aspect on the other. Therefore, they're known as a union. For this reason, many Dzogchen and Mahamudra teachings describe the nature as "unimpeded." The nature is an unimpeded, clear, transparent, lucid state. That is the nature of your present mind. Right now this fresh, present mind is in that state. When you see that, or when you experience that, it means that mind is seeing the mind. Mind is seeing mind itself. When you behold and maintain that recognition, you're in the natural state. There is nothing to contrive or structure. Just simply relax. Relax and be in that state. That's what the Dzogchen teachings always say.

There's a very famous Kagyu master known as Bengar Jampal Zangpo. In his teachings, he says, "Relax straight forward in the natural state. There's nothing to do. There is no action—no activity at all. Just simply relax straight forward in that natural state. When you're relaxing in that state, there's nothing to hold and nothing to grab. That is the way to abide and the way to continue this nature."

This meditation of relaxing in the natural state of mind is also known as the "Union of Shamatha and Vipashyana." When you're relaxing in that state, you're not separating anything; actually you're fulfilling both Shamatha and Vipashyana at the same time. That's why the great master Tsele Natsok Rangdrol says, "When the mind is free from moving and free from distraction, that aspect of the mind is Shamatha meditation." While you're abiding in a state of non-distraction, during that time, suddenly or naturally a thought will come. With continued awareness, you'll immediately recognize or see that thought coming. At that moment, if you look at the thought, it instantly dissolves into the clear, void, natural state without leaving any imprint. Therefore, Tsele Natsok Rangdrol says that when great practitioners are meditating, the moment a thought comes they immediately see it, and by looking at it, that same instant the thought dissolves without any destination. The instantaneous dissolving into the free, natural state is Vipashyana. That state of openness and freedom is Vipashyana.

During this way of meditating, both Shamatha and Vipashyana are in union. In other words, the abiding, stable aspect of the meditation is Shamatha, while the clear, emptiness aspect of the mind is Vipashyana, and both are in the same state. In Dzogchen terminology, when you continually abide in rigpa, the calm, abiding aspect of your meditation is Shamatha, and the *nature* of that calmness is free from any kind of existence or any categories, and that itself is the Vipashyana state. If we continually relax in the nature of mind with more clarity and in a relaxed way, uniting those aspects together is known as the "supreme seeing" of Vipashyana meditation.

When we reach this state we should avoid getting sidetracked during our meditation. If meditators always emphasize stabilizing the mind—always trying to stop thoughts or forcefully prevent them from arising—that's not the correct way to meditate. Blocking thoughts is a type of meditation, but according to the Buddha's Mahamudra and Dzogchen teachings, it's a very regular, ordinary, and worldly meditation. Meditating by blocking the mind has some benefits, but it won't uproot our negative emotions. It won't uproot grasping or bring liberation.

Meditation techniques that block thoughts are quite popular in non-Buddhist schools. In ancient times, there were many sages who practiced that way and built up a lot of mental stabilization using those techniques. When you block thoughts, it definitely reduces gross thoughts to a subtler state, and you can stay totally absorbed in that subtle state of conception, which does bring a lot of benefits and good qualities. It's very special and powerful because it reduces very dense, gross emotions and negativities. It almost settles them down to the lowest level, breaking heaps of emotions down to the subtlest levels. It's very, very special. However, it will not uproot our negative emotions and grasping. It won't uproot samsara.

There's a very famous Indian master named Ashvaghosha, who was a grand disciple of Nagarjuna, as well as a close disciple of Aryadeva. He's renowned for his poetry that praises the Buddha and all the different levels of the Buddha's extraordinary teachings. In one of his many praises to the Buddha's teachings, he said, "Those who have not met your teachings may actualize very absorbing, subtle states, and they may even reach the highest, deepest level of absorption in samsara. Yet because they can't break through that, they come back again to samsara. Therefore your teaching, which breaks through samsara, is extraordinary. I praise you."

During meditation, try to avoid forceful meditation. It's said repeatedly in the teachings: meditate more naturally. Don't make effort. Relax and calmly abide in the natural state. Then we're uniting both Shamatha and Vipashyana, and we'll continue to develop.

CHAPTER 12

FRAMING YOUR PRACTICE WITH THE THREE NOBLE ONES

Longchenpa

Whether we are engaging in the general teachings of Buddha Shakyamuni or the skillful means practices he taught in the Vajrayana, we should always uphold the "three frames" or "three structures" of practice, which are also known as the "three noble ones," or "three excellences" [*dam pa gsum*]. These include an excellent beginning, excellent middle, and excellent end of practice. We always begin with the preliminary or foundation practices, followed by the main or essential practices, which are then completed with the concluding practices.

The great Dzogchen master Longchenpa said, "Bodhichitta is the foundation, practicing without grasping and discursive thoughts is the main practice, and dedication and aspiration prayers are the conclusion." This was often quoted by Venerable Khenchen Palden Sherab Rinpoche and he always taught within these three frames. This means that motivation and intention are vital ingredients determining how our practice will transform us. To restrengthen our beautiful intention is therefore very important.

1. Noble Beginning (preparation)
    a. Refuge
    b. Bodhichitta

2. Noble Middle (main practice)
    a. Calm Abiding (Shamatha or Visualization Practice)
    b. Insight (Vipashyana or Dzogchen Meditation)

3. Noble Conclusion
   a. Dedication Prayers
   b. Aspiration Prayers

In order to insure that our practice stays on the path, we start by reflecting upon our precious life in this world and the beautiful consequences and situations that surround it. Then, through joy, devotion, and trust we call upon the lineage teachers who embody all the masters—Buddha Shakyamuni and Guru Padmasambhava— with devotional prayers.

With this as the starting point and the heart of our meditation, we engage in the main practice according to the lineage instructions we have received.

When our session has concluded we secure and seal our practice by dedicating the merit to all living beings with joy, bodhichitta, and vast aspiration prayers for an ever-increasing multitude of benefit and happiness. This seals our practice with a good heart.

The beginning is good, the middle is good, and the end is good. In this way, our practice will be perfect and beautiful from start to finish, and we'll have followed exactly in the footsteps of the ancient great masters.

CHAPTER 13

A SIMPLE MEDITATION PRACTICE

Seven-Point Posture of Buddha Vairochana

It is exceptionally helpful to meditate everyday at a regular time that is convenient for you. Early morning is ideal. In addition to your daily individual meditation, it's also very good to meditate with others.

Shrine

A shrine is a special place to sit and meditate. Set up a shrine in a permanent place that is appropriate for you. The shrine table should be covered in maroon or golden fabric. On the back of the shrine place an image or statue of the Buddha on a small, elevated platform covered in a dark blue cloth. If you don't have the space or your living situation doesn't allow for more, you can simply use a candle. Be realistic and harmonious with those sharing your living space. Your shrine symbolizes the enlightened universe of the Buddha and the true nature of your own mind, so with respect and mindfulness, always keep it clean and maintain a peaceful atmosphere around it.

Posture

The most important part of your posture is to keep your spine straight, but not rigid. Feel strong and grounded, but also very open, flexible, and relaxed. The teachings say, "Straight body, straight channels, straight winds, straight mind." Straightening your body naturally aligns your subtle energy channels, which calms your wind energies, and in turn balances your mind.

To do this, it's ideal to follow the traditional Seven-Point Posture of Buddha Vairochana:

1. Your legs can be in full lotus, half lotus, or cross-legged. If this is too difficult, perhaps a kneeling bench will help. If none of these are comfortable, use a chair that allows you to have a straight back with your feet firmly on the floor.
2. Your back should be straight but relaxed.
3. Rest both hands on your knees, or place your hands in the "Equanimity Mudra" with your right hand on top of your left hand with thumbs lightly touching each other, held at your navel. Gently pull your belly slightly in.
4. Hold your arms in the "Vulture Wing Position," with your shoulders back, chest open, and elbows held slightly away from your body.
5. Keep your neck straight, in line with your spine. Hold your head erect as though it was suspended by a string attached to the top of your head. Keep your chin slightly tucked in toward your chest.
6. Your tongue touches the roof of your mouth. Breathe normally.
7. Your eyes look down in front of you off the tip of your nose, with your eyelids semi-closed.

It's very helpful to have a supportive cushion or seat. Sit on a cushion that has the right height and firmness for you. Higher cushions are better if you have tight legs, and your knees will be slightly lower than your hips, which will support the natural posture of your spine. If a cushion isn't comfortable for you, try a kneeling bench or chair. It's most important to have a straight spine. If sitting on the floor is so uncomfortable that it continually interferes with your meditation, use a chair. If you're wearing pants, loosen the waistband for more relaxed breathing. Be gentle with your body.

MOTIVATION

In addition to your body posture, it's even more important to have the proper motivation. Think about these "four thoughts" that turn your mind towards your true nature and away from mistakenly relying on what is not reliable:

1. The preciousness of human life
2. The fragility of human life and the transitory nature of all things
3. Choosing beneficial actions and avoiding harmful actions
4. The inherent suffering of conditioned existence

Feel the preciousness of this opportunity with great joy and appreciation. Courageously begin your meditation with a very uplifted state of mind that is filled with bodhichitta: the sincere wish to help all beings be free of suffering and attain enlightenment. After taking refuge in the buddhas and the enlightened nature of yourself and all beings, practice with mindfulness, joy, and appreciation, as well as compassion and kindness for everyone—including yourself. Create a peaceful atmosphere that doesn't disturb others.

CALM ABIDING
(MEDITATION WITH A FOCUS)

With a very uplifted motivation, begin the main part of your practice by calming your mind—focus on an object of meditation such as your breath. Be mindfully present as you breathe in and out.

Thoughts will naturally arise, but gently yet firmly continue bringing your attention back to your breath. Let your mind rest attentively on the chosen object, and bring it back to this object when you notice you've become distracted. Do this for as long as you have time.

INSIGHT
(MEDITATION WITHOUT A FOCUS)

Next, while remaining present, relax your focus and rest in your natural state of mind without following thoughts about the past or future, calmly and peacefully abiding in the present moment with love, compassion, and wisdom. When you become distracted, without any questioning or judgment, bring your mind back to the present moment and again calmly rest there with joy. If you can, remain in that state for 10 to 20 minutes. Conclude with dedication prayers for the benefit of all beings.

In post-meditation, see everything as a dream-like magical display, and feel great joy and appreciation. Maintain this feeling throughout your daily activities.

DEDICATION

By this merit may all obtain omniscience.
May it defeat the enemy, wrong-doing.
From the stormy waves of birth, old age, sickness, and death,
From the ocean of samsara, may I free all beings.

At this very moment, for the peoples and nations of the earth,
May not even the names disease, famine, war, and suffering be heard.
But rather may pure conduct, merit, wealth, and prosperity increase,
And may supreme good fortunate and well-being always arise.

CHAPTER 14

THE FIVE STRENGTHS OF A DHARMA PRACTITIONER

AH Syllable

Our gracious, kind, and compassionate teacher Lord Buddha gave many different practice instructions. Among them were teachings on the five strengths: (1) devotion, (2) joyful effort, (3) mindfulness, (4) concentration, and (5) wisdom. With these five ingredients, we can keep our practice alive, and maintain, increase, and eventually cause our inner beauty to fully bloom.

DEVOTION

The first strength, devotion, is most important for practicing the Dharma. It is a combination of joy and appreciation for the Dharma, for oneself, and for our situation and circumstances, which didn't come together accidentally. All of these conditions are special, beautiful, and actually seldom occur. Devotion is the only way that we can open our hearts and motivate ourselves to practice.

Without devotion everything becomes very common, and we feel dull, useless, and depressed. We may even blame ourselves or our situation and circumstances, which eventually leads us to become victims of these emotions. Buddha Shakyamuni spoke many times about the importance of devotion. He said that devotion is like a door for light to come in, and a wheel with which to move to the enlightened state. Devotion increases all other good things.

Our situation and circumstances are precious, which means that time is also precious. Time is running like the Mississippi

River: even though we can't see it, the water is never standing still. Similarly, even though we can't see time, it's moving constantly. We should take full advantage of our existence to help ourselves and others. We can't fool around too much, playing games, experimenting, and missing opportunities. If we do that, we may end up leaving this world with some degree of regret, guilt, and self-blame. Instead, we should leave this world with joy, happiness, gratitude, and a sense of fulfillment. It's in our hands to leave the world in this way. Therefore, get up in the morning with joy and appreciation, during the day feel joy and appreciation and the preciousness of the teachings and your situation, and go to bed with joy, appreciation, and devotion. If you do this, the whole twenty-four hours of the day will become a beautiful state of joy, appreciation, acceptance, and patience, which will re-strengthen your spiritual qualities and practice.

JOYFUL EFFORT

Together with devotion we need joyful effort, which is the second strength. Effort is necessary because our laziness is crawling along behind us, very sneakily and quietly, so that sometimes we don't even see it until after it's already pulling us down. Laziness doesn't come forcefully. It's like the undercurrents in the ocean—strong and very persistent, undermining our goals and vision. We need uplifted, joyful effort to prevent laziness, but it shouldn't be effort that feels like a burden. To keep our effort joyful we should frequently think about the importance of our practice and our spiritual journey.

The Buddha pointed out three types of laziness: (1) general laziness, (2) habitual laziness, and (3) self-blaming laziness. With general laziness we're just not motivated. We feel heavy and dull and don't even want to move from our soft cushion except to push the TV remote or to get some popcorn and yummy drinks! We don't feel like doing anything—we just want to sit like a refrigerator watching television! This general laziness interferes with everything and we make no progress.

When general laziness happens, nobody is doing this to us—we're doing it on our own. Whenever we see ourselves in this situation, we should bring up devotion and joyful effort. We should think: "I'm falling into that ditch again. I'm wasting my time, my energy, and my circumstances." We should encourage ourselves and immediately lift ourselves up. If someone else tells us this, even if it's correct, we'll get upset. Therefore the Buddha said we should become teachers to ourselves.

With the second kind of laziness—habitual laziness—even if we're motivated to practice, we're more distracted by our old habitual pattern activities. We become obsessed with these habitual activities and don't practice or do good things that we want to do deep down in our hearts. We say, "I want to practice, but I have to clean the yard or watch a movie." Of course, we should do some things that we want to do, but spending too much time on them will not bring the result we're looking for. We have to be balanced and thoughtful.

The third laziness is self-blaming laziness, which is when we push ourselves down. Sometimes we make excuses for not doing what we want to do by saying, "I can't do that; I'm not good at it." Of course by using these excuses we can avoid practicing, and in the end they push us down and we become losers. Therefore, instead of self-blame we have to bring up courage and determination, joy and devotion, and say, "Yes, I can do it, I should do it, and I'm going to do it," and then make the effort.

Joyful effort supports the four other strengths, as well as the five other *paramitas* of transcendental generosity, morality, patience, concentration, and wisdom. It's like the wind that moves them. We have so many strong and pervasive habitual patterns that distract us from our principal purpose, so whatever our situation and circumstances—not just during sitting meditation—we should ignite joyful effort and devotion. If we have joyful effort throughout the day, we'll keep the Dharma continually in motion.

MINDFULNESS

The third strength is mindfulness, which also means thoughtfulness. It's intelligence or wisdom, opening and turning our radar in every direction. It's not a narrow state since it allows us to see all of our surroundings. Mindfulness is like a teacher, reminding us whenever we need it. It doesn't bother us like someone standing around saying we should do this and not do that. It's our inner intelligence, beautifully and gently giving us instructions, reminding us when we need it and then going back to the sidelines and standing by on duty.

Mindfulness also means remembering the instructions and teachings we've received from our teachers and read in books. We've gained a lot of knowledge, but without mindfulness we become absent-minded and forgetful. The knowledge printed in our alaya, or subconscious storehouse, sinks down almost as if it's gone. Without mindfulness, even if we've received teachings, the nugget instructions that are important to our practice and day-to-day lives are disabled.

Don't let the instructions sink down completely into the alaya. By recognizing their preciousness with joy and appreciation, bring them into the spotlight once in a while so they aren't hidden and can be applied. These instructions are guidelines for continually moving forward on our Dharma journey and for how we should act, speak, and think. If we have more mindfulness, everything will come quite easily and nicely—and not just for us! Our family, friends, and everybody else will also be happier and more comfortable. Mindfulness is even important for our health. On the practice level, mindfulness is like a wish-fulfilling jewel. It's the strength and the power of the practice.

CONCENTRATION

The next strength is concentration, which is another word for meditation. Up until now, devotion, joyful effort, and mindfulness have all been more outwardly oriented with emphasis on keeping up the instructions and practices. But concentration deals directly with the mind itself. The mind is so powerful—it rules our view, thoughts, speech, body, and environment. Usually the mind rules through the brain, which has become its big office or headquarters. Yet many of us are so distracted by our anxieties, emotions, and discursive thoughts arising one after another, that there's no leader guiding us in an organized way. We wake up in the morning with our mind jumping in different directions, and the whole day is spent like that until we finally go to bed. We may even sleep like that! That's why in Buddhism it's called "monkey mind;" a monkey's mind isn't very organized. It jumps in every direction, up and down, back and forth.

Concentration brings all those wandering anxieties and discursive thoughts into a more balanced order. The Buddha gave many different techniques for concentration, but they can be summarized into two types: Shamatha and Vipashyana. The type of concentration we're talking about here is Shamatha meditation. Shamatha is a Sanskrit word that means "calmly abiding." We're going to bring all those wandering discursive thoughts into a single state.

There are many different ways to practice Shamatha. If we're dealing with anger, we meditate on loving-kindness. When we have arrogance, we meditate on the six different elements—earth, water, fire, wind, space, and thoughts or conceptions. Arrogance is primarily the feeling of being superior, so by meditating on the six elements we see that we're all equal since we're made of the same six elements. If we have trouble with attachment, we should examine what we're attached to, dividing it into its component parts until we can rest our minds in the emptiness that we discover. Likewise, when we have problems with ignorance or dullness, we should bring up our knowledge of interdependent coordination—everything is related and nothing exists by itself. If we have ongoing discursive thoughts, we should meditate on our breathing. We can follow it like a thread all the way down to our ankles and back up to our nose, or as it comes in one nostril and goes out the other, or by counting our breaths from one to ten.

The most simple and widely used techniques for Shamatha are: (1) meditation with an object and (2) meditation without an object. For Shamatha with an object you can use a small statue of Buddha Shakyamuni and put it in front of you, looking at the level of his third eye. Bring your mind and eyes together and look to the point of the Buddha's third eye, almost creating a triangle, and just hold your attention there for as long as you can. With Shamatha without an object, you can simply relax or imagine an object. In Dzogchen teachings, you imagine a small, white AH syllable in a white sphere right on the tip of your nose, and then concentrate. You can either close your eyes or keep them open—whichever feels more comfortable.

If you have time to practice Shamatha meditation every day, maybe for fifteen minutes or a half an hour, begin with joy, appreciation, and devotion and feel the closeness and presence of the Buddha, Dharma, and Sangha. Then increase your bodhichitta, chant prayers, and meditate using one of the Shamatha meditation techniques for however much time you have. Keep up your practice with devotion, joyful effort, and mindfulness.

WISDOM

The fifth strength is wisdom, which is the knowledge of things exactly as they are, without understating, overstating, adding or subtracting anything. According to the Buddha's teachings, there are different levels of wisdom, such as understanding relative truth, absolute truth as it is, and how relative and absolute truth are combined without separation. The teachings also identify three types of wisdom: (1) wisdom that comes from studying, (2) wisdom that comes from contemplating, and (3) wisdom that comes from meditating and practicing. These are known as the "three wisdoms."

Our true nature is simple, easy, and gentle, but long ago our mind began twisting itself until it expanded and trapped us in a cocoon. The mind trapped itself—no one else did it to us. Similarly, our own creation of duality has trapped our intelligence, blurred our wisdom, and made things chaotic. Duality mind makes simple things complicated, and complicated things even more complicated.

Wisdom is simple and now we have to come back to that simple state. Because our habitual patterns are so strong and deep, like thick clouds in the sky, we have to clear them away and rediscover our true nature. In order to do this, the teachings say that it's good to study the *Tripitaka*, or Three Baskets: the Vinaya, Sutra, and Abhidharma teachings. When we study these three, we learn about morality and conduct, concentration and meditation, and the wisdom of the way things are. When you absorb these into your heart and mind, knowledge comes and opens your wisdom eye.

This kind of knowledge is called "certainty wisdom." In order for certainty wisdom to shine, we need to apply the second wisdom of contemplation. When we reflect on the meaning of the teachings, we have to use our own intelligence to refine what we've learned. The Buddha said, "Don't just take my word. You must examine and investigate for yourself." The certainty wisdom that comes from contemplation means that we no longer have doubt or hesitation, and we aren't worrying that this or that might happen.

Study and contemplation produce intellectual understanding,

but we won't realize the simple meaning of the nature of the way things are through intellect alone. We need to apply the third wisdom of meditation and practice, which will bring certainty wisdom to full bloom. Then we'll begin to see the nature directly with our inner wisdom eye—not just theoretically.

With the third wisdom, we meditate on what we've studied and contemplated. In Vajrayana, this wisdom meditation involves visualizing buddhas, chanting mantras, and engaging in Dzogchen meditation, all of which bring us closer to understanding the true nature. It's often said that in absolute meditation, we're resting in the state of simple, fresh, naked, ordinary awareness, coming back to the nature without exaggerating the way things are. Simply relax in the fresh, present moment state of the mind, and then meditate. This is Vipashyana Dzogchen meditation, which is also called "great emptiness meditation."

When we analyze things outside of us, we find the same thing as when we look within: emptiness. The *Madhyamaka* and Dzogchen teachings mention many times that the things we see are formations of heaps of atoms joined together. No single, substantially solid object exists. For example, if we examine a mountain, we eventually discover that it's just open, empty energy. There's no core, true existence. Right now it looks solid due to our habitual patterns and dualistic mind, but really it's a hallucination, an emptiness form. For that reason, the Buddha used the example of a field of grass: at first it looks like one solid green mass, but it's actually many individual blades of grass.

In terms of relative truth, objects are made of masses of atoms, and each atom has many particles that temporarily come together, but there's nothing solid. If we read books by great masters such as Nagarjuna, Mipham Rinpoche, or other great teachers from Tibet and India, we can see how they explored and analyzed every aspect of existence and discovered the nature of reality as it is. In a way, they were the first physicists. We can read and contemplate their teachings, but again, the final result of study and contemplation is practice. We have to practice in order to actualize the teachings.

According to Dzogchen pith instructions, start by simply relaxing into the present state of your mind and rest in that state. This is the entrance to discovering the nature of emptiness and appearances, and is commonly known as Vipashyana meditation. As we discussed before, Vipashyana is a Sanskrit word that means "supreme, extraordinary seeing," or "insight." We didn't recognize the true nature before, but now we're seeing it, which is wisdom.

If wisdom is applied with devotion, joyful effort, mindfulness, and concentration, then everything will be smooth and beautiful because all of the qualities of the nature are blended together perfectly. In order to maintain this vision, Buddha Shakyamuni, Guru Padmasambhava, and many great masters said many times: "See experiences as a dream, as magic, as a display." These teachers weren't just making this up. This entire world is a playful, magical display, including ourselves. Everything is in a beautiful, glorious, perfect state. Continually ignite this wisdom in your heart and mind, while constantly wishing good things for others. Stay down-to-earth, keeping up your good qualities and these Dharma practices. Be in the natural rhythm. This is known as being a practitioner.

Always conclude your practice with beautiful aspirations, dedicating the merit for all sentient beings to become enlightened now and in the future. Sincerely wish to remove all beings' suffering, difficulties, sicknesses, old age, loneliness, and whatever troubles they may be experiencing. Wish that they have an abundance of joy, happiness, and peace, and that they remain in that joyful state forever, fully discovering the enlightened natural state of their buddha-nature.

When we keep up these beautiful aspirations, we fulfill our

mission on this earth. If we leave this world with the beautiful attitude and fuel of the five strengths, we'll be lifted into the next stage, and this chapter of our lives will have been perfect and glorious. We will leave a legacy and example for others, and will move forward with a beautiful vision and goal.

CHAPTER 15

INTEGRATING STUDY AND PRACTICE

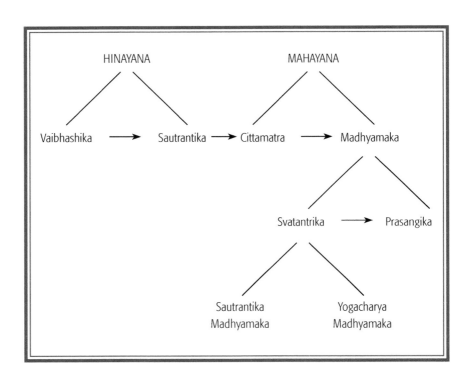

Buddhist Philosophical Schools

In order to maintain the Buddha's teaching, there are always two things that we need to do: (1) uphold the lineage of scripture, and (2) uphold the lineage of the *meaning* of that scripture. These are very renowned in Tibetan Buddhism as *shedra* and *drubdra*. Shedra is the teaching itself, which is kept up or maintained by drubdra, which is practicing the meaning of the teaching. In very simple terms, this is called study and practice, which always go hand-in-hand.

Again, in order to maintain the Buddha's teachings, we always put these two together—shedra and drubdra—the exact teaching itself along with the Three Wisdoms of study, contemplation, and meditation. In particular, we uphold the shedra, or study and contemplation aspect of the teachings in three manners. These are known as the three valid cognitions: (1) the valid cognition of direct perception, or *ngon sum tsedma*, (2) the valid cognition of inference, or *rjepag tsedma*, and (3) the valid cognition of establishing authenticity, or *yechi rjepag tsedma*.

In drubdra, we uphold the meditation aspect of the teachings in three manners known as (1) validation of the teaching by the Buddha, or *gyalwai ka tsedma*, (2) validation of the teaching by authentic lineage masters, or *gyudpai menngak tsedma*, and (3) validation using one's own awareness, or *rang gi rigpa tsedma*.

In other words, the first validation is that it is a teaching of the Buddha, which is correct. Based on that, the lineage masters share and explain the Buddha's teaching exactly according to their own knowledge. Thirdly, since the Buddha's teaching is valid and the lineage masters' explanation is also correct, then with your own study and contemplation, you absorb the teachings into your own heart and mind, and see that they're really true teachings. For the third validation you use your own inference techniques and evidence, because what you're investigating may be beyond what you're currently familiar with. This direct perception and true inference leads to confidence and trust in your own inner knowledge of the teachings.

For example, the Buddha said that during his past lives, over the period of time from Sangye Drenpa Yulkhor Chong to Sangye Namparzig, he contacted 55,000 buddhas and did practices, received teachings, and he never got bored or tired. In this world today, we don't have an exact proof of that. However, through trusting the words of the Buddha, by looking ourselves and comparing all the teachings from the Hinayana all the way to the Vajrayana, by reading his words, statements, and investigating whether there are any contradictions, we can see that there are no contradictions. Everything falls perfectly into it's own place, and each and every level activates a deeper understanding of meaning. Step-by-step, the teachings keep moving forward. The principal words in every teaching look perfect, therefore we can count on the Buddha's words.

Without the proper causes and conditions, realization and achievement couldn't happen. We can see this by using the evidence of causes, conditions, and their results. If we look at the world, it's obvious that no result comes without causes and conditions. So we can put all that together as an overview, which is this third valid cognition—the evidence we ourselves gather and use to prove that something is true. We come to an understanding, "everything is correct, therefore this must be true."

Everything has causes and conditions. Developing realization like the Buddha doesn't just come by itself. Therefore, we should keep working on our practice and meditation, continually following our role models: Buddha Shakyamuni, Guru Padmasambhava, and all those great masters of India and Tibet. If we keep up our joyful effort and expand our love and devotion as they did, we have every right and opportunity to achieve a similar realization. That's what they taught, others have proven it to be true, and that's also what we can see in the relative world. If the causes and conditions are perfect, there's no way to stop the result from developing. No way José! There is no way that we will not get the result. If the causes and conditions are perfect, the result will come as evidence. That's the truth. We can't deny it. That's the way things are. Therefore take the teachers of this truth as role models!

To do that, we have to study and practice. Again, studying the academic level of the scriptures is shedra, and practicing and applying the meaning of what you're studying through meditation is drubdra. In the Nyingma school of Tibetan Buddhism, we have the great opportunity to combine these two together. As our great teacher Khenchen Palden Sherab Rinpoche highlighted so many times, the Nyingma school doesn't separate study and practice— both are combined together without separation. Both are in union. During practice times you're studying, and when you're studying you're also practicing. It's not like east or west, in or out, up or down. Study and practice are always joined together, which is known as the union of practice and study.

In Tibetan, this is called *shedrup zungdrel*. *Shepa* is studying, and *drupa* is practicing. *Zungdrel* is translated as "joined together," or "union." When we combine these together with joy, appreciation, and humility, and with simplicity, respect, and appreciation, carrying a heart filled with bodhichitta, kindness, and compassionate thoughts, and reflecting that in our actions—deep down, that is practice. Therefore with humility, respect, and an open mind, we're moving forward—not staying in the past. Practice means we're looking to the future and moving forward with vision, with a goal, and with the bright, open eyes of wisdom. We're activating our inner beauty and the beauty that surrounds us, continually expanding our realization and moving forward.

That is the hallmark and identity of a practitioner—not being closed, tight and forced. At the very beginning when the Buddha gave his first teaching to the five disciples, he taught: "Our way is not that of an ascetic, nor is it luxurious—the middle way is our way." The middle way is the natural way. It's not just "our" way—it's the way of the nature. That's how everything develops. For example, when you look at external objects, it's only when causes and conditions are perfectly balanced that results develop. If anything is too extreme, the result won't come. We won't get the fruit. Ask plant nurseries how to produce good flowers and fruits—with balance, and by harmonizing all the necessary conditions. That is how we grow.

CHAPTER 16

EVERYTHING IS MIND

Magical Display

In Mahayana and Vajrayana Buddhism, the first thing to realize is that everything you see, everything you hear, and everything you think is none other than your own mind.

Intellectually maybe you think you already know this, but that's not enough—you have to settle this realization into your heart. You can't just hear it and say it and leave it at that. It must sink into your heart and mind until you see all perceptions as mind—your seeing is your mind, your hearing is your mind, and your thinking is your mind. It is yours and nobody else owns it, forced it, or threw it on you.

When you see beautiful things, your seeing and your thoughts of them are your mind. In the same way, high, low, big, small, good, and bad—every conception—as well as whatever you hear or perceive with your eyes, are all the baggage of your mind. If you see dirt, it is your mind. If you see "clean," it is your mind. Likewise if you feel pain, sorrow, or happiness, it is your mind. One hundred percent of appearances and whatever you think about them is your mind. Therefore, the moment you look at the world, see it as a display of your mind.

If you think about it, our conceptions aren't stable or something we can really rely on. They aren't firm because they are duality, and duality is deluded. Therefore, conceptions aren't perfect. In the early part of our lives we may have believed in something 100%, thinking it was absolutely perfect. Yet later in life we might completely refute this and adopt the opposite idea. So what happened? Who did that? It was none other than mind. Deluded mind is simply not reliable. If we think something is 100% beautiful and then change our mind 100% the other way, it's clearly not real. Every creation and division comes from our deluded, unreliable mind. The Dzogchen and Vajrayana teachings say that the first thing practitioners must realize is that all appearances and everything they hear and think is their mind.

We may wonder where all the stones in the earth come from. They come from atoms, which come from subatomic particles . . . which come from emptiness. Each particle is in the state of emptiness. Trees are emptiness, stones are emptiness, and mountains are emptiness because they're all constructed from emptiness. Everything is empty—including our ignorance and perceptions of duality. Our intellectual knowledge doesn't see it this way exactly, but that's the reality, whether we believe it or not. Our experience is structured by our conceptions, names, and labels, which we turn into compounded things. Yet if we look deep down, we find that these names and labels come from the mind. For this reason, the *Prajnaparamita* teachings say, "Form is emptiness, and emptiness is form."

When we look at the world itself, we only see three things reflected outwardly and inwardly. Everything we experience is form, sound, or empty space. If we understand the meaning of our body, speech, and mind, and use them in the right way, not only can we begin to transform ourselves and this body that we think is ours, but also the whole universe.

What are we purifying with our practice? We're purifying our clinging and the habitual tendencies of our body, speech, and mind. We're not trapped in samsara because we have a body, speech, and mind. We're caught because we *grasp* on to our body, speech, and mind. This clinging is what locks us in samsara.

Things appear according to how the mind perceives them. The more attachment we have for an object, the more it will be attractive to us. The more fear we have for an object, the more it will appear frightening to us. Even in this very short lifetime, we have already accumulated many habitual patterns. However, according to Buddhism, there is not just this life. We've accumulated habitual patterns life after life for countless aeons. Over time, these habitual patterns become very dense, strong, and concrete.

We have three different kinds of habits: (1) habits of how we perceive the whole world or universe, (2) habits of how we perceive the objects of our five senses, and (3) habits related to our body. These are also called: (1) habits of objects, (2) habits of the subject, and (3) habits of using one's own body, respectively. Of these three, the first habit includes things that are far away, the second includes things at a medium distance, and the third includes things that are very close. By purifying all of these habits, we begin to see the purity nature of the mind.

Knowing that all appearances are mind is very important. We need to look closely at this point and realize it ourselves. This realization is what will completely break our ego fabrication, our perceptions of duality, and our clinging to things as solid and existing. This is what Dzogchen is pointing out. It undermines the solidity of the ego and loosens grasping to subject and object by pointing out that all appearances are our mind. Duality mind is unreliable and always moving, therefore appearances are not reliable or fixed. Everything is flexible.

CHAPTER 17

REVEALING THE BUDDHA WITHIN

Buddha Maitreya

"Buddha-nature," or *tathagatagarbha* is the "seed," "essence," or "power" that enables us to attain enlightenment. All beings possess this extraordinary power. Whether human, cockroach, worm, lion, or elephant—we all have this special energy or cause of enlightenment. Every being also has this buddha-nature in equal measure. Insects and human beings, the rich and poor, males and females—whatever their state of existence or class of being—everyone possesses this potential in the exact same amount.

Considering the differences between a human being and a cockroach, you may have doubts about whether this is true or not. However, there really is no difference in their buddha-nature. The *ultimate* nature of a cockroach is the same as a human being. It's the same for enlightened beings and sentient beings as well—the only difference is to what degree the buddha-nature is obscured. Sentient beings have obscurations while buddhas do not. On the ultimate level, however, there's no difference between the buddha-nature of an enlightened being and the buddha-nature of a sentient being.

The Buddha gave many teachings in the Mahayana sutras stating that all beings equally possess the same essence of buddhahood. There are many ways to examine whether this is true. In the *Uttaratantra*, the great protector Buddha Maitreya taught the "three ways of reasoning" to logically prove that all beings possess buddha-nature, the true nature of mind. In general, Buddhism explains that all phenomena have three characteristics or principles: (1) causes and conditions; (2) the result of these causes and conditions; and (3) the nature, or identity of being dependently arisen and empty of inherent existence. Everything in both samsara and nirvana depends on causes and conditions, produces results, and has the nature of emptiness.

Maitreya's first reasoning is that by examining a result, you can know its cause. For example, if you look at a crop of corn or a harvest of apples, you can reasonably infer that they have arisen from a seed. Each one came from a seed in relation to the kind of fruit it produced. If you examine the life of Buddha Shakyamuni, you will see that at one time he was an ordinary being like us, but through practice he achieved buddhahood. In the same way, all sentient beings have the cause by which they can achieve buddhahood. This is an example of looking at the result to prove that sentient beings have the inherent cause of buddha-nature.

The second reasoning involves looking at the ultimate nature of the way things are. In Buddhism, this is often referred to as emptiness, or *shunyata*. By relying on this, one will see that the ultimate nature is all-pervasive and resides within all sentient beings, as well as the Buddha. When we say "ultimate nature," what exactly does this refer to? It is the original nature of great emptiness, which is pure from the beginning and inseparable from clarity. Since profound, great emptiness is pervasive to everyone and never changes, regardless of whether we recognize it or not, all beings are able to achieve enlightenment.

The third reasoning is that enlightened beings possess complete, supreme knowledge and have attained the ultimate degree of loving-kindness, compassion, and power. They have revealed 100% of their buddha-nature. Although sentient beings possess some of these qualities, they haven't yet developed them to the fullest extent. We all have the causes and conditions to develop buddha-nature to our full potential in the same way a mango seed can develop into a tree. The seed which develops into buddhahood includes loving-kindness, compassion, and great emptiness. These qualities are the very nature of our minds. By recognizing and maintaining these innate qualities within ourselves, we will eventually bring them to full realization. Seeing that we do already possess some degree of the qualities of buddha-nature is the third reasoning.

After we establish without a doubt that all beings possess the seed of buddhahood, we can then determine that the reason we don't recognize our ultimate nature is because we're temporarily deluded by the two obscurations of negative emotions and confusion. Buddha-nature is like the sun, and obscurations are like clouds that cover the sun. Are the sun and clouds the same? No—clouds only temporarily obscure the sun; they arise suddenly and disappear suddenly. When clouds cover the sun and then disperse, we know that the sun and its rays didn't reappear from somewhere else. The sun was always there, but the clouds temporarily obscured it. In the same way, obscurations temporarily cover our buddha-nature. Once they're purified, it's not as if our buddha-nature suddenly arrives from some other place—it was there all along.

If all sentient beings didn't already have buddha-nature they would not be able to attain enlightenment. If you press sand trying to get oil out of it, you won't be able to. If you take charcoal and try to wash the black color out of it, you'll never succeed. Yet because sentient beings do possess buddha-nature, if they practice and accomplish the teachings of the Dharma by purifying their obscurations, they will eventually achieve enlightenment.

Once we establish that all sentient beings have this exceedingly precious nature filled with infinite goodness qualities and without any faults, we have to *realize* it through meditation. The essence of our buddha-nature is emptiness, and its nature is luminous clarity. It possesses all positive qualities, is without any flaws, and has always been inseparable from us. Through the course of our existence, we have constantly fluctuated between happiness and suffering. Yet our buddha-nature is unchanging and without fault.

At the end of this epoch, the entire world will be destroyed by fire and water, but the sky will not be affected—it always remains constant. Buddha-nature is like the sky—no matter what happens, it doesn't change.

If we actualize our full potential and attain buddhahood, we reveal the supreme wisdom that has the capacity to instantaneously know everything in the past, present, and future. The loving-kindness and compassion of a buddha doesn't make distinctions between self and others—it is all-pervasive compassion. This is the supreme attainment and it will never revert back to samsara. It is forever free of sorrow and hardship. It is bliss and the true nature of reality.

CHAPTER 18

TANTRA: THE ENLIGHTENED NATURE OF OUR BODY, SPEECH, AND MIND

Guru Padmasambhava

All of the teachings of the Buddha are designed to purify our obscurations and remove the suffering of ourselves and others. That is the single purpose of the teachings of the Buddha. As you know, the Buddha didn't just give one teaching, and he didn't act like a king or an emperor, ordering us to blindly follow his teaching and that's it. Buddha Shakyamuni laid out many categories and levels of teaching according to the particular needs, desires, intelligence, and sensibilities of practitioners. In response to these differences, the Buddha gave a wide variety of teachings that were specifically suited to the unique characteristics of individuals. In this way, the Buddha skillfully ensured that all beings could benefit from the Dharma. But despite the inconceivably vast scope of these instructions, the purpose of each one is the same: to remove the obscurations and suffering of all beings and reveal our innate nature, which is the nature of everything.

These teachings can be summarized in many different ways. According to the Nyingma school of Tibetan Buddhism, the 84,000 teachings of the Buddha can all be summarized in terms of the nine yanas [*theg pa*], or levels of study and practice. They are:

Foundational Buddhism
    (1) Shravakayana, or "Hearer Vehicle"
    (2) Pratyekabuddhayana, or "Solitary Realizer Vehicle"

Mahayana
    (3) Bodhisattvayana, or "Bodhisattva Vehicle"

Vajrayana: Outer Tantras
>   (4) Kriyayogatantra, or "Action Yoga Tantra"
>   (5) Upayogatantra, or "Dual Yoga Tantra"
>   (6) Yogayogatantra, or "Yoga Tantra"

Vajrayana: Inner Tantras
>   (7) Mahayogatantra, or "Great Yoga Tantra"
>   (8) Anuyogatantra, or "Subsequent Yoga Tantra"
>   (9) Atiyogatantra, or "Supreme Yoga Tantra"

According to the Nyingma classification, the first two yanas are known as "Foundational Buddhism," or "Hinayana," and all the rest of the levels—from the 3rd through the 9th—are known as "Mahayana." The Mahayana is divided into Sutra Mahayana and Tantra Mahayana, or Vajrayana. Sutra Mahayana is the 3rd level, while the Vajrayana includes everything from the 4th level of Kriyayoga up to and including the 9th level of Atiyoga, or Dzogchen. Levels four through six—Kriyayoga, Upayoga, and Yogayoga—comprise the Outer Tantras, while yanas seven through nine—Mahayoga, Anuyoga, and Atiyoga—make up the Inner Tantras.

These different categories of teachings don't contradict or suppress one another. Each of the teachings is designed to explore the nature as it is more closely. As we said before, the intention of every teaching is the same: to reveal the nature and to remove the obscurations and suffering of all beings, so there isn't really any difference regarding their purpose.

So then what is the difference between these teachings? Often the teachings list three differences: (1) the degree of clarity, (2) details, and (3) completeness. For example, the lower, more foundational teachings are not as clear, detailed, or complete. As you go higher and deeper, the teachings become more clear, more detailed, and more thorough and complete. When you reach Dzogchen, or the levels of the Inner Tantras, the teachings are completely clear, completely detailed, and completely thorough. At the beginning level teachings, such as the Shravakayana, the teachings tell us the same thing, but they're a little more brief, not as detailed or clear, and not so thorough. Yet this way of teaching is very suitable for certain individuals. It's what they're able to comprehend and digest, and therefore the teachings follow that. But otherwise, all of the teachings are the same and follow the same purpose of discovering the innate nature and removing suffering.

When we practice the teachings, they lead us to a more pure state of the nature because we purify our obscurations. When we purify our obscurations, our body becomes more pure, our speech becomes more pure, and our mind becomes more pure. Then we begin to discover the purity state of the nature—the way things are when they're not covered up by our obscurations. This is how we progress through the nine yanas.

According to the system of the Tantra Mahayana, or Vajrayana teachings, the phenomena of samsara and the phenomena beyond samsara both have the same nature, without any exception. In other words, we can briefly say that the Vajrayana view sees that both samsara and nirvana are inseparable in the body mandala, speech mandala, and wisdom mind mandala of the Buddha without any distinctions or divisions. Within these three mandalas, both samsara and nirvana are already enlightened or already divine. They're already this way. This isn't something that's developed through our practice or through our path right now. Everything is already in this state. This is the essential, condensed teaching of the Inner Tantras: everything is already within this enlightened state. This is what we have to practice and realize through our meditation.

We should really think about this: how is the body already in the state of enlightenment? How is speech divine? And how is the mind naturally enlightened? All appearances are perceptions and conceptions. If this is true, then what is body? Usually we think that "body" refers to our physical body, which is true. But in this case, "body" means everything that has mass, or all the forms that we see through our eye. All tangible objects are considered body or form. And most of the time, what is it that perceives forms? Usually, our eye perceives forms and often it's said that form is the object of the eye consciousness. In a more logical or technical way, we can say that everything with solidity is form. In the end, it doesn't matter exactly how many different categories of form we make. Who really perceives and conceptualizes all of these forms? It's our own mind.

Usually we think of speech in terms of our voice or the words of others. It's true that this is also speech, but here "speech" refers to all sound systems. Every sound system is included in the category of speech. And again, who perceives and conceptualizes these sounds? It is none other than our own mind.

Of course mind includes things such as thinking, recollecting, reflecting, and all of our ideas and intelligence. All of these are definitely mind. But here, the vast, spacious nature of everything is considered mind. The infinite quality of space—and even beyond space—is mind. And who perceives this infinite nature? Who conceives of space? That spacious, infinite nature is none other than our mind.

If we look at each of these categories of body, speech, and mind, we'll find that there's nothing permanent, tangible, or solid that exists in any of them. Body, speech, and mind are totally in the vastness state of emptiness. Whether we think about something, hear it, or see it doesn't matter. There aren't any special, essential distinctions that separate these three categories. All forms, sounds, and thoughts share the same nature of emptiness. And since everything is included in body, speech, and mind, everything is emptiness.

This nature of emptiness wasn't created just now. The Buddha didn't create it before and neither did any of the other great lineage masters. The nature of reality is originally empty since beginningless time. Therefore it's called the originally enlightened state, free from duality, and free from grasping and clinging. The nature doesn't become enlightened through our practice. We don't make it pure through the process of meditation—it's already enlightened.

We are trying to connect our mind to the nature as it is, without any interference by duality or grasping. The nature is perfectly pure and free from all duality. In the Vajrayana, this pure nature is called the deity or divine. This divine nature is not just a figure that we visualize. Most of the time these images are just our duality mind. But the nature of reality is totally pure. When we see this nature with pure perception, we realize that everything is really divine. Everything is the pure, original nature as it is.

CHAPTER 19

DZOGCHEN:
THE GREAT PERFECTION

Transcendental Wisdom Rainbow Body of
Guru Padmasambhava

By practicing Dzogchen with joyful effort, courage, commitment, and devotion, we can reach enlightenment within this single lifetime. We are very fortunate to have connected to this powerful teaching and have the opportunity to discuss and practice it.

Dzogchen is not just the highest teaching in and of itself—it is the highest teaching because it is supported by and includes all the other yanas. That's why it is called "Great Completion" or "Great Perfection." When we practice Dzogchen, we're engaging all the other teachings of the Buddha as well, including the "Hinayana," Mahayana, and Vajrayana. Hinayana is completely included within Mahayana; Mahayana and Hinayana are included within Vajrayana; and Hinayana, Mahayana, and Vajrayana are all included within Dzogchen. Dzogchen is very rich and profound. The Buddha combined all the teachings together into a single vehicle of practice, and that is the great path that all the ancient masters and practitioners followed to reach supreme enlightenment.

We are following the very same path. We're not trying to select just one thing or another from the teachings and disregard the rest. When we discriminate between teachings, or accept and reject this or that part of the Dharma framework, we're not following the teachings of the Buddha and Guru Padmasambhava.

We must incorporate all three yanas—the Hinayana, Mahayana, and Vajrayana—into our practice, rather than choose among them. This same message was passed down by all the ancient masters—our teachers—who followed this path and achieved realization. For example, there is no higher realization than that of Guru Padmasambhava, yet he followed the exact same instructions he is giving us. He too followed the Hinayana, Mahayana, and Vajrayana teachings given by Buddha Shakyamuni. Guru Padmasambhava said that he was a follower of Buddha Shakyamuni. He followed every single word of the Buddha's teachings, and honored and appreciated them everywhere he went.

Keeping this in mind, we should also remember that whenever we study and practice the teachings of the Buddha, we should have great courage, commitment, and joyful effort for putting them into practice and letting them mature in our hearts and minds. We shouldn't just let them hover intellectually in our brains.

Of course it's important to use our intellect to analyze and investigate, but the true nature of Dzogchen will never be found by the intellect. Our nature is beyond the intellect. Intellectual investigation and analysis are conceptions. Even if they are good conceptions that help us understand better, they can never explore the true depth and meaning of Dzogchen. After we analyze, we must learn how to relax and go beyond analysis.

This is not only true for Dzogchen. Nothing that deals with absolute truth can be discovered with intellectual conceptions and philosophies. Mahamudra, Madhyamaka, and Prajnaparamita, as well as Sakya *Lamdre* [*lam 'bras*] teachings on Path and Result, the Six Application Practices of the Inner Tantras known as *Jordruk* [*sbyor drug*], and the Kalachakra teachings all deal directly with absolute truth, and absolute truth cannot be discovered through conceptual mind or its manipulations. For this reason, all the teachings of the Buddha and the great masters say in a single voice: discover your true nature without altering it or providing any structure or framework. Go beyond analysis and conception. The moment you go beyond conception, you're in the absolute, authentic, open, natural state of freedom.

In one of the Mahayana sutras, the great compassionate Buddha said to a god requesting a teaching, "Absolute truth is not subject to word, name, or label, nor is it subject to any of the activities of body, speech, and mind. If it is, it is not absolute truth—it is relative truth." This means that whenever we're trying to do something or hold something, it's not the absolute true nature spoken about by the Buddha or pointed out in Dzogchen.

Similarly, the great master Shantideva said in the 9th chapter of the *Guide to the Bodhisattva's Way of Life*, "Absolute truth is not subject to conception. If it is, it is relative truth." Shantideva cut through very precisely and completely to the truth, giving the perfect description without any hesitation. Clearly and perfectly he said, "The subject of conception is relative truth. Absolute truth does not depend on conception." This message is clear and bright—we can all hear and understand this.

In Dzogchen, absolute truth is discovered by the two famous techniques of (1) Kadak Trekcho and (2) Lhundrub Togal. Both of these teachings go beyond all conceptions and imagination.

In the Dzogchen practice of Kadak Trekcho, *kadak* means "pure from the beginning," and *trekcho* means "cutting thoroughly." But what does "cutting thoroughly" and "pure from the beginning" actually mean? Who is doing the cutting? It is none other than our own rigpa. What is rigpa? Rigpa is not duality, it is not fabrication, and it is not conception—rigpa is beyond all of these. When we relax in rigpa, we're relaxing beyond conceptions and their fabrications. Rigpa is beyond all ideas. Therefore rigpa is known as original, authentic wisdom. Throughout the Dzogchen teachings there are many other terms used to describe rigpa, including the "nature of mind," "original mind," "original wisdom," "unfabricated mind," and "self-born wisdom."

When we're practicing Dzogchen meditation, what we are meditating on? We're maintaining the authentic nature of rigpa. That is our meditation. Rigpa is always with us. It has never left us even for a second. That's why Dzogchen meditation requires no big, forceful effort. The teachings always say to just relax in the nature. Abiding in the nature is very soothing and restful, like cruising down an open highway. If we can rest in our nature without being carried away by the window wipers of conception, then we're really settled in our original nature. At that moment we begin to discover the beauty, calm, peacefulness, gentleness, vastness, openness, and freedom of the absolute truth. We not only discover it, we're in it, and it is part of us.

When we relax in the natural state, conceptions begin arising due to our habitual patterns. If we are very established in Dzogchen, those arising conceptions are nothing bad actually. They're not an enemy or an obstacle. They are the expressions of rigpa. Arising thoughts and conceptions are part of rigpa—they have the same nature. The rigpa we experience as relaxing, free, and calm is the same nature as arising thoughts. Rigpa and thoughts are never separate; both are the same. If we don't manipulate arising thoughts with our habitual patterns and duality, they will self-liberate into the dharmakaya. Guru Padmasambhava said, "If you leave the arising movement of thought alone, it instantly becomes a dharmakaya display." In describing how arising thoughts instantly dissolve into the dharmakaya, other teachings use the metaphor of snow falling into a lake. The moment the snow touches the lake, it melts and becomes the same as the water. There is no difference between them.

With a good foundation in rigpa through Trekcho meditation, we then practice Togal to discover the deeper beauty of rigpa. The practice of Togal involves visions, but what are the visions really? They are the dense arising power of rigpa reflecting itself externally. We begin to behold our inner nature in the outer display.

How should we think of rigpa? Rigpa is beyond conception, but it is also full of light and wisdom. It's not like a black hole or blank emptiness. It is full of clarity and luminosity. Rigpa is why we can perceive all the objects of our five senses—why we can see, hear, and touch everything. All of this is because rigpa is magnetizing and can communicate with external objects. It is like a light that clears everything up so we can see precisely, clearly, and perfectly, without blocking or mixing anything up. Rigpa can be reflected in many ways: as forms, lights, colors, and sounds. Through Togal we begin to instantly discover this richness. We call them "visions," but they aren't hallucinations. They are visions of our original, inherent nature.

CHAPTER 20

JOY AND APPRECIATION
ARE REALIZATION

Buddha Samantabhadra

Without joy and appreciation our practice won't go very far. Even if we receive nugget teachings like Dzogchen and Mahamudra, without appreciation and devotion our practice becomes dry. There's no moisture. It's like dropping a seed in the desert—it will just dry up and won't grow. But if you plant that same seed in a nice field with good soil, moisture, and other beautiful conditions, it will definitely grow. Joy and devotion are like fertilizer for the seed of our buddha-nature. Feeling joy, appreciation, and devotion are really important.

We should always begin our practice with joy and devotion, refuge and bodhichitta. The essence of joy, devotion, and refuge is confidence. Have confidence in the Buddha, Dharma, and Sangha. The essence of bodhichitta is love and compassion, having kind thoughts for others, and even just feeling "kind-hearted," "joyful-hearted," "compassionate-hearted," and "appreciation-hearted." If we feel these beautiful qualities, our practice will be a piece of cake. It won't be a difficult, boring, dragging practice, where we think, "Oh, I have to practice. I *have* to do this or I *need* to do this." When our practice is dragging like this, what we might be lacking is joy, devotion, and bodhichitta, or confidence and love. If we have all these beautiful qualities, everything comes together so perfectly. That's why His Holiness Dudjom Rinpoche says, "I bow down respectfully and take refuge." In other words, I have trust, confidence, and joy.

In India they sometimes call this surrendering. You surrender yourself. We're not going to resist by clinging and giving all the power to our egos and habitual patterns. We're going to give power to the Buddha, the Dharma, and the Sangha by surrendering to the practice. Think, "I am not going to resist this." When we surrender, it doesn't mean we're losing anything. Deep down, what is losing? Ego-clinging. Our ego and arrogance are losing. The ego always thinks, "I want it to be this way, *my* way, *my* style. You don't fit with me. I don't like that." Of course we can think this way, but when it comes to our practice, if we keep doing this, what will happen over time? We'll lose the ground of our practice, of the Dharma, and who wins? Our ego-clinging and negative habitual patterns of attachment, grasping, and clinging win. They'll gain the upper hand. In order to avoid this, it's very important to feel respect, appreciation, and trust. Take refuge at the feet of the glorious, supreme guru.

Taking refuge at the "feet of the guru" doesn't mean you're going to actually touch your teacher's feet. In ancient times when they prostrated to the teacher or the shrine, they always touched the lowest part of the shrine. They didn't jump up to the head of the Buddha, but placed their head at the Buddha's feet. This means the highest part of their body touched the lowest part of the object of refuge. Honoring the Buddha's feet means having less arrogance in our heart. We should feel deep reverence when we practice. Some of you may have seen that even in India today, many times younger people touch the feet of their elders in order to show respect. They respect their knowledge and experience, and appreciate their guidance. This is how the lineage tradition of the past has survived and developed a very rich culture.

When we have less arrogance, we learn. Arrogance is a big obstacle. The teachings always say this, and we can experience it for ourselves. Arrogance is like an iron ball—no matter how much water you pour on an iron ball, it won't hold the water. Similarly, when you have arrogance, no matter how much knowledge you learn from others, it won't sink in. It just spills out. Therefore, with respect we bow down to the lotus feet of the teacher and take refuge.

You may be wondering about Dzogchen realization, which is beyond all effort and duality. It's true—Dzogchen realization is the highest realization and the ultimate goal. It is the perfect and complete recognition of the already enlightened nature of ourselves and everything. But at this point, realization is something we have to think about more practically, in a more tangible way, according to what we can handle right now. Dzogchen realization begins with what we've been discussing: joy, devotion, and bodhichitta. These qualities *are* realization. When we realize these qualities in our hearts, Dzogchen and Mahamudra realization comes so easily. For this reason, the great master Saraha said, which Khenchen Palden Sherab Rinpoche often quoted: "Realization comes by accumulating merit and receiving blessings from the teacher." Blessings from your teacher come from devotion. When we have devotion, joy, and appreciation, accumulating merit becomes the bodhichitta practice of the six paramitas. As many of you know, there are two accumulations: merit and wisdom. We have to accumulate both merit and wisdom for our realization to be complete. Once both of these come together, realization naturally comes.

Realization itself *is* joy, devotion, bodhichitta, confidence, and compassion. If we have these, our soil is activating, spring is coming, and our buddha-nature is definitely growing. Realization will come. These qualities are the springtime display of the energy of realization. Joy, devotion, and bodhichitta are the dawn of realization. They are realization, and will inevitably lead to full bloom realization. When we chant or meditate, we pray: "May joy be born in my heart. May loving-kindness and compassion be born in my heart. My devotion be born in my heart. May confidence and trust be born in my heart." That is the path of profound realization.

"Profound" means that your love is infinite, your joy is infinite, and your devotion is infinite. That's what we have to realize. For some of us our joy, devotion, and bodhichitta may be shallow. Our love, kindness, and compassion may be shallow as well. They aren't profound enough. We haven't reached the depths of our nature yet. When we activate and touch the profound depths of our nature—that is actually the path. We are moving forward inwardly, deepening our practice and meditation. Realization begins to come so nicely and quickly when we reveal these deep qualities of our nature, and then the realization of Dzogchen and Mahamudra that we've been talking about and looking for all the time is not far away. It's just there. It comes so surprisingly and beautifully, almost unexpectedly.

When we read the life stories of the great masters who achieved such high realization, they all went through what sounds like a very long and difficult process, but their courage and commitment, and immense joy and devotion were unyielding and unfailing. Their devotion continued no matter what happened, and then realization came instantly with some simple technique. Sometimes it almost sounds ridiculous when we hear how they got realization. How could it happen that way? It happened because they continued to deepen their joy, devotion, bodhichitta, and confidence, and at some point their realization burst forth and they became a sky yogi, merging with Buddha Samantabhadra, Buddha Shakyamuni, and Guru Padmasambhava. After a long time of looking and longing for realization, it just happens in an instant. Their entire journey started with and depended on their joy and devotion, bodhichitta and confidence, and their firm commitment. You can read about this in so many biographies that are translated into English now. Eventually these practitioners became totally fearless and enlightened, yet so simple and beautiful. Beginning each practice with these qualities will quickly bring about realization of the profound path without any errors or mistakes.

In the teachings you often read about people saying, "I got

so much realization." I've also heard this many times. They'll say, "I got so much realization, but I don't know what it is." (Khenpo Rinpoche laughs to himself.) That must be a very skeptical, doubtful realization. They don't know what their realization is, and I don't know either!

When true realization comes there's no need to doubt it or be skeptical about it. It's like a brilliant sun rising in the sky, free from clouds, mist, dust, and pollution. It's just brilliant! You feel happy and confident. You feel glorious, and yet so gentle and peaceful, filled with love and kindness. When we read about great masters like Buddha Shakyamuni and Guru Padmasambhava, their realization is like that. In order to develop "doubt-free," certain, unerring realization, we start with joy, devotion, and bodhichitta, and move forward with that. It's so beautiful. We don't have to be skeptical about joy. We don't have to be skeptical about devotion. We don't have to be skeptical about loving-kindness and compassion. They are so brilliant and true, so special and beautiful, and they bring full realization that is also so beautiful and special. That's what it says throughout the Buddha's teaching.

When we fully realize the "primordial citadel" of our true nature, we'll have no fears. We won't be scared of anything and we won't hope for anything. We'll have no hope, no fear, no expectations, and no longing. We will have achieved everything, and therefore the Dzogchen teachings say—and we've heard this from Khenchen Palden Sherab Rinpoche and many siddhas so many times—we will be full of confidence and fearlessness. When you achieve the highest Dzogchen realization, even if you see millions of buddhas right in front of you, there will be nothing more to ask and nothing more to receive. You already got everything. Similarly, even if you're surrounded by millions of enemies, you will have nothing to fear. You will have discovered your original nature, naked and fresh without being covered up by anything. That is what is known as "receiving blessings."

DEDICATION OF MERIT

May the victory banner of the fearless teachings
of the Ancient Tradition be raised.

May the victorious drum of the teaching and practice of Dharma
resound in the ten directions.

May the lion's roar of reasoning pervade the three places.
May the light of unequalled virtues increase.

* * *

Dharmapalas who made commitments
to the lamas of the three lineages,

Dharmapalas of the three groups,
summon up your superior mighty powers.

Help quickly disseminate throughout the three worlds,

The treasure of the pure Dharma lineages
of the three enlightened beings.

* * *

May all the temples and monasteries,
All the readings and recitations of the Dharma flourish.
May the Sangha always be in harmony,
And may their aspirations be achieved.

* * *

At this very moment, for the peoples and nations of the earth,
May not even the names disease, famine, war, and suffering be heard.
But rather may pure conduct, merit, wealth, and prosperity increase,
And may supreme good fortune and well being always arise.

APPENDICES

Acknowledgments

The Samye Translation Group would like to thank everyone who was involved in helping to bring this project to fruition. In particular, we would like to thank Amanda Lewis for compiling and editing this book.

Thanks also to Lama Pema Dragpa for his final review, and for helping coordinate the layout and printing process. We thank Ann Yegorova for her work on cover and book design, and Michael Nott for his work on the final stages of production.

Venerable Khenchen Palden Sherab Rinpoche and Venerable Khenpo Tsewang Dongyal Rinpoche gave these teachings over a period of more than thirty years. We thank everyone who helped with each of the chapters.

Introduction: Finding Everlasting Joy, Peace, and Happiness

Teachings by Ven. Khenpo Tsewang Dongyal Rinpoche from the 2012 Dzogchen Summer Retreat at Padma Samye Ling on Guru Dragpo according to the lineage of Tsasum Lingpa on July 17, 2012

Transcribed by Ross Hathaway
Edited by Amanda Lewis

Chapter 1: What is Buddhism Really About

Teachings by Ven. Khenpo Tsewang Dongyal Rinpoche from the 2016 One Month Dzogchen Retreat at Padma Samye Ling on Lama Shabkar Tsokdruk Rangdrol's *Flight of the Garuda*, Year 3 on May 3, 2016

Transcribed by Andrew Cook
Edited by Mary Ann Doychak, Lama Pema Dragpa,
and Amanda Lewis

CHAPTER 2: THE FOUR NOBLE TRUTHS OF LIFE

Teachings by Ven. Khenchen Palden Sherab Rinpoche and Ven.
Khenpo Tsewang Dongyal Rinpoche from the 2006 One Month
Dzogchen Retreat at Padma Samye Ling on Vimalamitra's Nyingthik
teachings on March 12, 2006
    Transcribed by Veda Alban
    Edited by Amanda Lewis

CHAPTER 3: DISCOVERING A RELIABLE REFUGE

Teachings by Ven. Khenchen Palden Sherab Rinpoche and Ven.
Khenpo Tsewang Dongyal Rinpoche from the 2006 One Month
Dzogchen Retreat at Padma Samye Ling on Vimalamitra's Nyingthik
teachings on March 12, 2006
    Transcribed by Veda Alban
    Edited by Amanda Lewis

Teachings by Ven. Khenpo Tsewang Dongyal Rinpoche from the
public talk "What It Means to Be a Lay Buddhist" at Tashi Choling
on September 21, 2014
    Transcribed and Edited by Amanda Lewis

CHAPTER 4: THE FOUR THOUGHTS
THAT TURN THE MIND TOWARD THE DHARMA

Teachings by Ven. Khenpo Tsewang Dongyal Rinpoche from
the 2012 One Month Dzogchen Retreat at Padma Samye Ling
on Karma Chagme's *Union of Mahamudra and Dzogchen* on

April 9, 2012
  Transcribed by Linda Bland
  Edited by Mary Ann Doychak and Amanda Lewis

CHAPTER 5: BREAKING THE CYCLE OF SUFFERING: THE TWELVE LINKS OF INTERDEPENDENCE

Teachings by Ven. Khenpo Tsewang Dongyal Rinpoche from the 2015 PSL Shedra at Padma Samye Ling on Nagarjuna's *Letter to a Friend* on August 28, 2015
  Transcribed by Turtle Hill Sangha
  Edited by Craig Bialick and Amanda Lewis

Teachings by Ven. Khenchen Palden Sherab Rinpoche and Ven. Khenpo Tsewang Dongyal Rinpoche on the "Heart Sutra According to the Vajrayana View" given in Naples, Florida in 2001.
  Transcribed by Iris Flowers
  Edited by Eduardo Sierra and Amanda Lewis

CHAPTER 6: JOURNEY TO AWAKENING: THE NOBLE EIGHTFOLD PATH

Teachings by Ven. Khenpo Tsewang Dongyal Rinpoche from a public talk at Yeshe Tsogyal Temple in Nashville, Tennessee on June 5 and 6, 2013
  Transcribed by Melina Sierra and Tracy Moore
  Edited by Amanda Lewis

CHAPTER 7: THE FOUNDATION OF THE SPIRITUAL PATH

Teachings by Ven. Khenpo Tsewang Dongyal Rinpoche from the 2011 One Month Dzogchen Retreat at Padma Samye Ling on His Holiness Dudjom Rinpoche's *Mountain Retreat Instructions* on

April 1, 2011
>Transcribed by Karen Johnson Feltham
>Edited by Amanda Lewis

CHAPTER 8: DISTINGUISHING BENEFICIAL ACTIONS FROM HARMFUL ACTIONS

Teachings by Ven. Khenpo Tsewang Dongyal Rinpoche in New York City in 1981
>Transcribed by Richard Steinberg
>Edited by Eduardo Sierra and Amanda Lewis

CHAPTER 9: SHARPEN YOUR WISDOM WITH THE THREE TRAININGS

Teachings by Ven. Khenchen Palden Sherab Rinpoche and Ven. Khenpo Tsewang Dongyal Rinpoche on Mipham Rinpoche's *Wheel of Analytic Meditation* at Padma Gochen Ling in Monterey, Tennessee in the early 2000's.
>Transcribed by Michael White and Greg Leaming
>Edited by Michael White, David Cowey
>and Lama Pema Dragpa

CHAPTER 10: STAYING ON TRACK WITH MINDFULNESS

Teachings by Ven. Khenchen Palden Sherab Rinpoche and Ven. Khenpo Tsewang Dongyal Rinpoche from the 2006 One Month Dzogchen Retreat at Padma Samye Ling on Vimalamitra's Nyingthik teachings in 2006, edited for the Spring/Summer 2008 PBC Pema Mandala magazine
>Transcribed by Jane Gilbert
>Edited by Sujata Ghosh, Andrew Cook,
>and Amanda Lewis

CHAPTER 11: HOW TO MEDITATE

Teachings by Ven. Khenchen Palden Sherab Rinpoche and Ven. Khenpo Tsewang Dongyal Rinpoche on Karma Chagme's *Lamp of Mahamudra* at Padma Samye Ling on July 29 and 30, 2008
>Transcribed by Deana Bodnar and Brian Anderson
>Edited by Jane Gilbert and Amanda Lewis

CHAPTER 12: FRAMING YOUR PRACTICE WITH THE THREE NOBLE ONES

Written by Ven. Khenpo Tsewang Dongyal Rinpoche at Mandarava House on the 3rd day of the Month of Miracles in 2011
>Transcribed and edited by Lama Laia Pema Tsultrim

Teachings by Ven. Khenchen Palden Sherab Rinpoche and Ven. Khenpo Tsewang Dongyal Rinpoche during the 2009 Shedra on Anuyoga at Padma Samye Ling on September 2, 2009
>Transcribed by Larry Jones
>Edited by Andrew Cook

CHAPTER 13: A SIMPLE MEDITATION PRACTICE

Written by Ven. Khenpo Tsewang Dongyal Rinpoche at Mandarava House in 2015, and excerpted from "Opening the Door to Tibetan Buddhism"
>Transcribed and edited by Lama Pema Dragpa

CHAPTER 14: THE FIVE STRENGTHS OF A DHARMA PRACTITIONER

Teachings by Ven. Khenchen Palden Sherab Rinpoche and Ven. Khenpo Tsewang Dongyal Rinpoche to the PBC Tampa Bay Sangha on March 13, 2011

Transcribed and edited by Jane Gilbert
and Lama Pema Dragpa

CHAPTER 15: INTEGRATING STUDY AND PRACTICE

Teachings by Ven. Khenpo Tsewang Dongyal Rinpoche from the 2011 PSL Shedra at Padma Samye Ling on the nine yanas on September 1, 2011
Transcribed and edited by Amanda Lewis

CHAPTER 16: EVERYTHING IS MIND

Teachings by Ven. Khenchen Palden Sherab Rinpoche and Ven. Khenpo Tsewang Dongyal Rinpoche from the 2002 Three Month Dzogchen Retreat at Padma Samye Ling on *Yeshe Lama*
Transcribed by Celia Barnes
Edited by Clint Sidle, Elizabeth Gongde,
and Lama Pema Dragpa

CHAPTER 17: REVEALING THE BUDDHA WITHIN

Teachings by Ven. Khenpo Tsewang Dongyal Rinpoche in New York City in 1981
Transcribed by Richard Steinberg
Edited by Richard Steinberg and Amanda Lewis

CHAPTER 18: TANTRA: THE ENLIGHTENED NATURE OF OUR BODY, SPEECH, AND MIND

Teachings by Ven. Khenchen Palden Sherab Rinpoche in 1987 at the Kagyu E-Vam Buddhist Institute in Australia
Transcribed by Kagyu E-Vam Buddhist Institute
Edited by Lama Pema Dragpa and Amanda Lewis

Chapter 19: Dzogchen: The Great Perfection

Teachings by Ven. Khenchen Palden Sherab Rinpoche and Ven. Khenpo Tsewang Dongyal Rinpoche from the 2002 Three Month Dzogchen Retreat at Padma Samye Ling on *Yeshe Lama*
    Transcribed by Celia Barnes
    Edited by Clint Sidle, Elizabeth Gongde,
    and Lama Pema Dragpa

Chapter 20: Joy and Appreciation Are Realization

Teachings by Ven. Khenpo Tsewang Dongyal Rinpoche from the 2011 One Month Dzogchen Retreat at Padma Samye Ling on His Holiness Dudjom Rinpoche's *Mountain Retreat Instructions* on March 28, 2011
    Transcribed by Patty Ibur
    Edited by Amanda Lewis

As always, we are deeply grateful to Lama Jomo Lorraine, Lama Laia Pema Tsultrim, and Lama Pema Dragpa for their joyful and steadfast administrative help with the Padmasambhava Buddhist Center. Along with them, we would like to thank all the resident staff of Padma Samye Ling in New York, whose work actively supports the Venerable Khenpo Rinpoches' activities both locally and internationally. We sincerely appreciate all members and friends of the Padmasambhava Buddhist Center worldwide for their constant participation and enthusiasm over many years.

Most importantly, we offer our heartfelt gratitude and devotion to the Venerable Khenpo Rinpoches for blessing us with the opportunity to receive and practice these profound teachings. We request that Venerable Khenpo Tsewang Dongyal Rinpoche continue to turn the wheel of Dharma, and offer many sincere prayers for his long and healthy life. We also pray for the long and healthy life of the reincarnation of Venerable Khenchen Palden Sherab Rinpoche.

We sincerely ask the forgiveness of all wisdom beings, lineage holders, and readers for any and all errors and misinterpretations of the teachings present in this text, and we welcome suggestions on how to improve it in the future. May everyone who reads this understand the value and meaning of their precious human life, and may their highest aspirations be fulfilled for the benefit of all beings!

LIST OF ABBREVIATIONS

CE   Khenchen Palden Sherab Rinpoche and Khenpo Tsewang Dongyal Rinpoche. *Ceaseless Echoes of the Great Silence: A Commentary on the "Heart Sutra Prajnaparamita."* Edited by Joan Kaye, Phyllis Taylor, and Andrew Cook. 3rd edition glossary by Andrew Cook. Sidney Center, NY: Dharma Samudra, 2012.

DIF   Khenchen Palden Sherab Rinpoche and Khenpo Tsewang Dongyal Rinpoche. *Discovering Infinite Freedom: The Prayer of Küntuzangpo.* Edited by Ani Joanie Andras, Robert Hulton-Baker, Cynthia Friend, and Carl Stuendel. Sidney Center, NY: Dharma Samudra, 2010.

EJLD   Khenchen Palden Sherab Rinpoche and Khenpo Tsewang Dongyal Rinpoche. *The Essential Journey of Life and Death, Volumes 1 and 2.* Edited by Lama Pema Dragpa, Amanda Lewis, Craig Bialick, Michael White, and Ann Helm. Sidney Center, NY: Dharma Samudra, 2012.

GI   Compiled by Yudra Nyingpo and other disciples. *The Great Image: The Life Story of Vairochana the Translator*, translated by Ani Jinba Palmo. Boston: Shambhala, 2004.

HEC   Khenchen Palden Sherab Rinpoche and Khenpo Tsewang Dongyal Rinpoche. *Heart Essence of Chetsun: The Voice of the Lion.* Edited by Andrew Cook with Lama Pema Dragpa. Sidney Center, NY: Dharma Samudra, 2007.

IP   Khenchen Palden Sherab Rinpoche and Khenpo Tsewang Dongyal Rinpoche. *Illuminating the Path: Ngondro Instructions According to the Nyingma School of Vajrayana Buddhism.* Edited by members of the Samye Translation Group: Craig Bialick, Ann Helm, James Fox, and Clint Sidle. Sidney Center, NY: Dharma Samudra, 2008.

IT   Reginald Ray. *Indestructible Truth: The Living Spirituality of Tibetan Buddhism.* Boston: Shambhala Publications, 2000.

KPSR   Khenchen Palden Sherab Rinpoche.

KTDR   Khenpo Tsewang Dongyal Rinpoche.

LDWD   Khenchen Palden Sherab Rinpoche and Khenpo Tsewang Dongyal Rinpoche. *Liberating Duality with Wisdom Display: The Eight Emanations of Guru Padmasambhava.* Edited by Craig Bialick, Lama Pema Dragpa, and Amanda Lewis. Sidney Center, NY: Dharma Samudra, 2012.

LFIW   Khenpo Tsewang Dongyal Rinpoche. *Light of Fearless Indestructible Wisdom: The Life and Legacy of His Holiness Dudjom Rinpoche.* Prose translation and annotation by Khenpo Tsewang Dongyal & Carl Steundel. Verse and song translation by Toy-Fung Tung & Marie-Louise Friquegnon. Ithaca: Snow Lion Publications, 2008.

NSTB   His Holiness Dudjom Jigdral Yeshe Dorje. *Nyingma School of Tibetan Buddhism: Its Fundamentals and History.* Translated by Gyurme Dorje and Matthew Kapstein. Boston: Wisdom Publications, 1991.

OWDMS   Khenchen Palden Sherab Rinpoche and Khenpo Tsewang Dongyal Rinpoche. *Opening the Wisdom Door of the Madhyamaka School.* Edited by Andrew Cook and David Mellins. Sidney Center, NY: Dharma Samudra, 2007.

OWDOT   Khenchen Palden Sherab Rinpoche and Khenpo Tsewang Dongyal Rinpoche. *Opening the Wisdom Door of the Outer Tantras: Refining Awareness Through Ascetic Ritual and Purification Practice.* Edited by Andrew Cook. Sidney Center, NY: Dharma Samudra, 2008.

PONM   Khenchen Palden Sherab Rinpoche and Khenpo Tsewang Dongyal Rinpoche. *Pointing Out the Nature of Mind: Dzogchen Pith Instructions of Aro Yeshe Jungne.* Edited by Richard Steinberg with Lama Pema Dragpa. Sidney Center, NY: Dharma Samudra, 2012.

RPJK   Ringu Tulku. *The Ri-me Philosophy of Jamgön Kongtrul the Great: A Study of the Buddhist Lineages of Tibet.* Boston: Shambhala, 2006.

RYG   Rangjung Yeshe Online Glossary. <http://www.rangjung.com/rootfiles/ryp- glossary.htm>.

RYW   Rangjung Yeshe Wiki, "Dharma Dictionary." http://rywiki.tsadra.org/index. php/Main_Page.

SPG   Khenchen Palden Sherab Rinpoche and Khenpo Tsewang Dongyal Rinpoche. *Splendid Presence of the Great Guhyagarbha: Opening the Wisdom Door of the King of All Tantras.* Edited by Andrew Cook, Lama Pema Dragpa, Keith Endo, and Amanda Lewis. Sidney Center, NY: Dharma Samudra, 2011.

TBD   Guru Padmasambhava, revealed by Terton Karma Lingpa. *The Tibetan Book of the Dead* (*Great Liberation By Hearing In The Intermediate States*), translated by Gyurme Dorje. New York: Penguin, 2006.

WN   His Holiness Dudjom Jigdral Yeshe Dorje. *Wisdom Nectar: Dudjom Rinpoche's Heart Advice*, translated by Ron Garry. Ithaca: Snow Lion, 2005.

WPT   Dza Patrul Rinpoche. *The Words of My Perfect Teacher*, translated by the Padmakara Translation Group. Boston: Shambhala, 1998.

Skt.   Sanskrit.

Tib.   Wylie transliteration of the Tibetan.

GLOSSARY

Abhidharma [Skt.; Tib. *mngon pa*]. One of the Three Baskets (*Tripitaka*), the other two being the Vinaya and the Sutras. The word *Abhidharma* is alternately translated into English as "directly cognizing" or "vividly seeing" [*abhi*] the teachings [Skt. *Dharma*], or "about the teachings." This implies that an individual directly sees the Dharma, without exaggeration or imagination. The Abhidharma includes teachings on Buddhist psychology and logic, descriptions of the universe, steps on the path to enlightenment, different kinds of beings, and refutations of mistaken beliefs. CE. See also **Sutras, Three Baskets**, and **Vinaya**.

alaya [Skt; Tib. *kun gzhi*]. The "all-ground" or "subconscious storehouse" is literally translated as "foundation of all things." It is the basis of mind and both pure and impure phenomena, and all karmic imprints are stored here. In some cases *alaya* is a synonym for buddha-nature or the dharmakaya, the recognition of which forms the basis of all pure phenomena. In other cases, *alaya* refers to the neutral state of duality mind that has not been recognized as innate wakefulness. In this latter case, the alaya forms the basis for samsaric experience. RYG.

arhat [Skt; Tib. *dgra bcom pa*]. Literally "foe-destroyer," this term refers to beings who have conquered the "enemies" of the afflictive emotions by realizing the nonsubstantiality of the self. They are free from the suffering of samsara. Nonetheless, arhats fall short of complete buddhahood until, after death, they are eventually roused from samadhi and trained in the Mahayana path as bodhisattvas. Arhathood is the goal of the Hinayana, or foundational Buddhist teachings. CE. See also **Hinayana**.

asura [Skt.; Tib. *lha min*]. Also known as anti-god or demi-god, a being in one of the three upper realms of samsara who is similar to the gods, but is constantly dominated by the emotional poison of envy, and always at war with the gods. DIF. See also **six realms**.

bhumi. See **five paths**.

bodhichitta [Skt.; Tib. *byang chub kyi sems*]. Literally, the "mind of enlightenment," comprising impartial love, compassion, and wisdom for all beings. *Relative bodhichitta* indicates the wish to attain buddhahood for the sake of all parent sentient beings by practicing the path of love, compassion, and wisdom. This itself can be divided into (1) "aspiring bodhichitta" and (2) "actualizing bodhichitta." The former indicates the altruistic intention to usher all sentient beings into the permanent state of enlightenment by achieving liberation oneself, whereas the latter indicates actually engaging in bodhichitta activities. In contrast, *absolute bodhichitta* is a synonym for the nature of mind, the open, vast clarity of awareness itself. Absolute bodhichitta recognizes that all beings are primordially enlightened—there is no liberator, no deluded beings, and no act of liberation, since nothing ever moves from the absolute sphere of the dharmadhatu, or rigpa. Abiding in this great immovable resting is the ultimate bodhichitta. It is always important to practice the union of relative and absolute bodhichitta. The Venerable Rinpoches often teach that if at first it is difficult to practice absolute bodhichitta, there is no need to worry—by practicing relative bodhichitta, the mind will gradually become more relaxed, peaceful, and open, eventually expanding into the ultimate state of absolute bodhichitta. CE, HEC, LFIW. See also **bodhisattva**.

bodhisattva [Skt.; Tib. *byang chub sems dpa'*]. Literally, "courageous one for enlightenment," a *bodhisattva* is an advanced Mahayana practitioner who traverses the five paths and ten bodhisattva levels (Skt. *bhumi*). Such a practitioner is so committed to working for the benefit and welfare of others that, on one level, he or she chooses to remain in samsara in order to bring all beings to full enlightenment. Practically speaking, however, they take relative and absolute bodhichitta as the essence of their practice and strive to attain complete enlightenment themselves, after which point they will be able to benefit beings much more effectively. See also **bodhichitta**.

buddha [Skt.; Tib. *sangs rgyas*]. The term *buddha* denotes one who has completely awoken from the fundamental ignorance of the two obscurations (i.e., conflicting emotions and knowledge) and developed unceasing pristine cognition of buddha-nature. Having cultivated every positive quality to its utmost limit, a buddha has traversed the bodhisattva levels and eliminated all obscurations to true knowledge. Thus, he or she enjoys the five fruitional aspects of a buddha: enlightened (1) body, (2) speech, (3) mind, (4) qualities, and (5) activities, or the "five wheels of inexhaustible adornment" [*mi zad rgyan gyi 'khor lo lnga*]. Buddha Shakyamuni was the fourth of one thousand buddhas that will appear during the current Fortunate Aeon. See also **Dharma** and **buddha-nature**.

completion stage [Tib. *rdzogs rim*] One of the "two stages" of Vajrayana practice, the other being the "creation stage." The completion stage focuses primarily on the vajra mind through one of two techniques: (1) the completion stage with characteristics and (2) the completion stage without characteristics. Examples of the first include Tummo, Dream Yoga, Phowa, Bardo, and other practices, also known as "skillful means practices." By visualizing and meditating on the actual, inherent qualities within our body, including our channels, winds, and essence elements, we discover great bliss-emptiness, the absolute Guru Padmasambhava. In all these practices, we hold, visualize, and concentrate on something. In the completion stage without characteristics, we don't concentrate on anything but simply rest in the fresh, present state and behold the panoramic view of outer and inner phenomena without any boundaries. Examples of this include the Dzogchen practices of Trekcho and Togal. EJLD, Vol. 1. See also **creation stage** and **Vajrayana**.

concentration [Tib. *ting nge 'dzin*; Skt. *samadhi*]. Concentration is one of the themes of the paramitas and the Noble Eightfold Path taught by Buddha Shakyamuni, which can be divided into teachings belonging to three categories: (1) *shila* [*tshul khrims*], ethical conduct; (2) *samadhi*, concentration associated with meditative equipoise; and (3) *prajna* [*shes rab*], transcendent wisdom. The Sanskrit word samadhi can be defined as "undistracted concentration," "mental focus," "meditative stabilization," "meditative absorption," "contemplation," "total involvement," "undividedness," and others. By cultivating concentration, we develop the power to bring the mind into a state of clarity and equanimity. The three categories of concentration are (1) worldly concentration, (2) concentration that goes beyond the world, and (3) concentration that benefits others. In the context of Vajrayana, concentration can refer to either the creation stage or the completion stage. CE, EJLD, Vol. 1. See also **completion stage**, **creation stage**, **Noble Eightfold Path**, **shila**, **six paramitas**, and **wisdom**.

creation stage [Tib. *bskyed rim*]. One of the "two stages" of Vajrayana practice, the other being the completion stage. The creation stage is related to Mahayoga, in which everything is seen as the indestructible body, speech, and mind of enlightenment, or the "three vajra states." Creation stage practice can be generally divided into (1) visualization and (2) mantra recitation. After we establish the visualization of the deities, we recite their mantra.

When we visualize our environment and ourselves as enlightened during Vajrayana practice, we are bringing out our inner, self-born awareness wisdom without being disturbed by duality and habitual patterns. We're discovering the splendid qualities of our inner primordial wisdom, which then shines out through our body and speech. Our body becomes primordial wisdom form and our speech becomes primordial wisdom sound. When the sunlight of our inborn nature of primordial wisdom shines through our speech and body, we're inseparable from Guru Padmasambhava. In fact, we *are* Guru Padmasambhava. Our nature of self-born wisdom awareness is absolute Guru Padmasambhava. EJLD, Vol. 1. See also **completion stage** and **Vajrayana**.

Dharma [Skt.; Tib. *chos*]. The Sanskrit word *dharma* has about ten different meanings, but here it refers to the teachings of Buddha Shakyamuni. In general, there are two aspects of the Buddhadharma: *transmission,* or teachings that are actually given; and the Dharma of *realization,* or the stages that are attained by applying the teachings. What distinguishes the Dharma as such is the presence of "four seals" or "four marks" [*bka' rtags kyi phyag rgya bzhi*] that separate worldly teachings from transcendent ones. These are often given as follows: (1) "all compounded things are impermanent," (2) "all afflictive emotions are of the nature of suffering," (3) "all phenomena are empty and devoid of a self-identity," and (4) "nirvana is peace" or "nirvana is beyond extremes." See also **buddha** and **tathagatagarbha**.

dharmadhatu [Skt.; Tib. *cho ying*]. The absolute expanse; emptiness pervaded with awareness. DIF. See also **dharmakaya** and **wisdom**.

dharmakaya [Skt.; Tib. *chos sku*]. Dharmakaya is the ultimate nature and essence of enlightened mind on the absolute level. When it comes to the relative level, it indicates the primordial purity of phenomena, related with the fact that all phenomena are equal in the state of great emptiness. The dharmakaya is uncreated, free from conceptual elaboration, naturally radiant, empty of inherent existence, and spacious like the sky. Although by its very nature it cannot adequately be expressed in words, the dharmakaya is the very suchness [Skt. *Tathatha*] that pervades all phenomena—all subjects, objects, and actions. CE. See also **nirmanakaya** and **sambhogakaya**.

dhyani. See **Five Dhyani Buddhas**.

Dzogchen [Tib. *rdzogs chen*; Skt. *Mahasandhi*]. Often translated as "Great Perfection" or "Great Completion," Dzogchen represents the highest teachings of Buddha Shakyamuni, comprising the ninth and last yana of the Nyingma school. The term "Great Perfection" can be understood to mean that all the Buddha's teachings are utterly complete and perfected in Dzogchen; thus, all nine yanas are encompassed, without contradiction, in this the pinnacle of every vehicle. The Dzogchen teachings were first brought to Tibet and taught by three principal masters: Guru Padmasambhava, Panchen Vimalamitra, and Vairochana. These teachings can be subdivided into three principal lineages: the Mind Class [*sems sde*], Space Class [*klong sde*], and Pith Instruction Class [*man ngag gi sde*]. Through the practice of Dzogpa Chenpo, all enlightened attributes are effortlessly perfected in one's own intrinsic, primordial awareness, known as *rigpa*. According to the Dzogchen teachings, the nature of awareness is empty in essence (dharmakaya), luminous in nature (sambhogakaya), and unconfined in capacity (nirmanakaya); moreover, these three characteristics are indivisible (svabhavikakaya). CE. See also **Nyingma**.

Five Dhyani Buddhas [Tib. *rigs lnga'i sangs rgyas*]. Sambhogakaya emanations of the dharmakaya buddhas Samantabhadra and

Samantabhadri, including (1) Vajrasattva [*rdo rje sems dpa'*], (2) Vairochana [*rnam par snang mdzad*], (3) Ratnasambhava [*rin chen 'byung gnas*], (4) Amitabha [*snang ba mtha' yas*], and (5) Amoghasiddhi [*don yod grub pa*]. SPG. See also **dharmakaya** and **sambhogakaya**.

Five Paths [Tib. *lam lnga*; Skt. *Pancamarga*]. (1) The accumulation path [*tshogs lam*] is characterized by strong devotion, unwavering confidence, and firm bodhichitta commitment. (2) The application path [*sbyor lam*] is marked by results grounded in the accumulation path, such as bodhichitta achievements. Devotion is deeply actualized in one's heart and actions, instead of being just a mental aspiration. (3) The seeing path (or "all-seeing path") [*mthong lam*] is the point of full realization, when great emptiness is seen as it is and the entire universe is perceived as the magical display of the true nature. Attaining this path brings forth utter satisfaction and great joy and corresponds to the first bhumi. (4) The meditation path [*bsgom lam*] continues from the seeing path to the point of deepest realization through meditation. True nongrasping merit is the result. This path includes the second through tenth bhumis. (5) The path of no more learning [*mi slob pa'i lam*] is the point of highest realization, when pristine buddha-nature is fully actualized. At this point, samsara and nirvana are equal, no more practice is needed, and great benefits can be accomplished for others. This path is the eleventh bhumi, or total enlightenment, depending on how one enumerates the bhumis (i.e., sometimes the tenth bhumi is subdivided into three or six additional categories, for a total of thirteen or sixteen bhumis). OWDOT. See also **bodhisattva**.

Four Noble Truths [Tib. *bden pa rnam bzhi*; Skt. *catvari aryasatyani*]. Initially taught in Sarnath, India, the Four Noble Truths comprise the first teaching given by the Awakened One after his enlightenment under the Bodhi Tree [*khyad par gnas*] in

Bodhgaya. They are respectively: (1) "the truth of suffering" [*sdug bsngal gyi bden pa*], (2) "the truth of the origin of suffering" [*kun 'byung ba'i bden pa*], (3) "the truth of the cessation of suffering" [*'gog pa'i bden pa*], and (4) "the truth of the path leading to the cessation of suffering" [*lam gyi bden pa*]. The Buddhist path is not possible without an understanding of these teachings, since they form the basis of all subsequent Dharma teachings. For instance, the Tathagata summarized his teachings in the following way: "I teach only two things: suffering and the way out of suffering."

Maitreya and many others compared the Buddha and the Four Noble Truths to the relationship between a doctor and his or her patient. To begin, the doctor must understand the symptoms of the patient—that is, the various types of afflictions he or she experiences. The doctor must then be able to diagnose the underlying cause(s) of the symptoms. Next, the doctor must know whether a cure is possible and, if so, the characteristics of the cure. Finally, the doctor must outline a path and prescribe the appropriate medicine to cure the illness. While the Four Noble Truths outline a perfect path, it is ultimately up to the patient to use the nectar-like medicine of the teachings properly in order to experience the desired result. So, the patient must (1) recognize the sickness, (2) discover the cause of that sickness, and (3) actualize the cure by (4) applying the proper remedy.

The Four Noble Truths are both profound and vast in scope. Among other things, they describe the three kinds of suffering, the nature of impermanence, the absence of a substantially-existent self, how grasping to this illusory self leads to continual suffering, dependent origination, samsara, nirvana, and the Noble Eightfold Path that leads to nirvana. All schools of Tibetan Buddhism share the "common preliminaries" or "four thoughts that turn the mind from samsara," which incorporate many aspects of the Four Noble Truths, particularly the truths of suffering and the cause of suffering. These reflections generally include: (1) recognizing of the preciousness of human life endowed with liberty and opportunity, (2) reflecting on the impermanent nature of all compounded things and conditioned states, (3) contemplating the inexorable workings of cause and effect, or karma, and (4) meditating on the nature of samsara as an ocean of suffering. The Vajrayana universally emphasizes the importance of these teachings, because genuine renunciation of samsara and its infinite suffering is not possible without deeply reflecting on the truth of these statements and taking them to heart.

His Holiness Dudjom Rinpoche explains that the Four Noble Truths pertain to the three times of past, present, and future, and are taught in twelve ways: "[1] suffering is this, [2] it can be diagnosed, [3] it has been diagnosed; [4] the origin of suffering is this, [5] it can be abandoned, [6] it has been abandoned; [7] the cessation of suffering is this, [8] it can be verified, [9] it has been verified; [10] the path to the cessation of suffering is this, [11] it can be developed and [12] it has been developed." IT, NSTB, TBD, WPT; KPSR and KTDR, PSL spring month-long retreat, March-April 2006. See also **buddha**, **Dharma**, **nirvana**, and **samsara**.

Hinayana [Skt.; Tib. *theg pa dman pa*]. Literally "Lesser Vehicle," this group of Buddhist teachings is so named because it focuses on individual enlightenment rather than that of all sentient beings. The Hinayana comprises the foundational Buddhist teachings of the Shravakayana and Pratyekabuddhayana. It emphasizes monastic discipline, strict meditation, contemplation of the Four Noble Truths, renunciation of the worldly distractions of samsara, and rigorous study of the twelve links of dependent origination, all of which eventually bring about the realization of the emptiness of self and thereby liberation from cyclic existence, known as *arhathood*. The principal philosophical views of the Hinayana are expounded in the Vaibhashika and Sautrantika schools. See also **arhat**, **Dharma**, and **Mahayana**.

hungry ghost [Tib. *yi dvags*]. See **six realms**.

karma [Skt.; Tib. *las*]. Literally, "action" or "activity," *karma* generally refers to volitional action, in which virtuous actions give rise to positive results and negative actions give rise to negative results. Karma is often classified as either "individual" or "collective." As the Rangjung Yeshe online glossary explains, "Distinction is made between collective karma, which defines our general perception of the world, and individual karma, which determines our personal experiences." The natural, unerring "law" of karma, or cause and effect, dictates that all volitional actions are causes which produce like results. Present experiences are largely based on past karma, whereas future experiences are based on both past karma and especially karma created in the present, though when and how karma ripens depends upon innumerable causes and conditions. CE.

Madhyamaka [Skt.; Tib. *dbu ma*]. The "Middle Way" philosophy of Buddhism. In their *Opening the Wisdom Door of the Madhyamaka School*, the Venerable Khenpo Rinpoches give a brief introduction to Madhyamaka in the following way:

> It is called the Middle Way because it is not extreme; Madhyamaka is not right wing or left wing. These are the ultimate teachings of the Buddha. In Tibetan Buddhist philosophy, this ultimate view is known as *ngedon* [*nges don*], literally "definitive truth." Ngedon refers to the certain, definitive, inevitable meaning of the nature as it is. Since there is nothing further to add and nothing to subtract from Madhyamaka, it is known as definitive. By directly referring to the nature as it is, Madhyamaka explains the ultimate meaning of truth, the nature of all things.... [T]he Buddha gave three or four seminal teachings known as the turnings of the wheel of Dharma. Madhyamaka comes from the second and

third turnings, and the Vajrayana teachings—sometimes known as the "fourth turning of the wheel of Dharma"—are based on Madhyamaka. Consequently, Madhyamaka is the essence of the Buddha's second, third, and fourth seminal teachings. Generally speaking, Madhyamaka comes from the *Prajnaparamita* teachings of the second turning of the wheel of Dharma.

Ringu Tulku adds, "All four schools of Tibetan Buddhism agree that Madhyamaka is the highest philosophy, whose nature is free from all extremes. To summarize Madhyamaka, one could say that the ground is the union of the *two truths* [absolute and relative], the path is the union of the two accumulations [merit and wisdom], and the result is the union of the two kayas [dharmakaya and rupakaya]." The differences between the various schools of Tibetan Buddhism relate to how the relative and ultimate truths are understood. On the whole, there are two different schools of Madhyamaka: (1) Svatantrika Madhyamaka, or *Rangyupa* [*rang rgyud pa*], and (2) Prasangika Madhyamaka, or *Thalgyurpa* [*thal 'gyur pa*]. These two schools present profound and sophisticated philosophical systems, both within the specific context of Buddhism and in the more general context of human history. Despite their subtle differences—as noted earlier—*all* Madhyamaka philosophy is characterized by freedom from the four extremes: (1) existence, (2) nonexistence, (3) both existence and nonexistence, and (4) neither existence nor nonexistence. Thus, although objects appear substantial, they are without inherent, substantial existence. OWDM, RPJK.

Mahamudra [Skt.; Tib. *phyag rgya chen po*]. Literally, the "Great Seal," Mahamudra is a profound Vajrayana practice for directly realizing buddha-nature. It is widely practiced by the Kagyu school of Tibetan Buddhism.

Mahayana [Skt.; Tib. *theg pa chen po*]. Literally, "Great Vehicle," the Mahayana teachings are characterized by the practice of the six paramitas, the cultivation of the altruistic intention to free all beings from the sufferings of samsara, and the active application of this intention in action or practice. These latter two are respectively known as "aspiring bodhichitta" and "actualizing bodhichitta." Including both sutras and tantras, the Mahayana is generally associated with the second, third, and fourth turnings of the Wheel of Dharma, which emphasize the inseparable union of wisdom [Skt. *Prajna*] and compassion [Skt. *Karuna*]. See also **Hinayana**.

mandala [Skt.; Tib. *dkyil 'khor*]. Literally, "center and surrounding," the term *mandala* usually refers to the enlightened environment of a buddha, or to a graphic representation of a tantric deity's realm of existence. There are three principal kinds of *mandalas*: (1) the intrinsically existent mandala (*svabhava-mandala*), not accessible to ordinary beings, which is the actual configuration of the qualities of enlightenment; (2) the meditational mandala (*samadhi-mandala*) as visualized by a tantric practitioner; and (3) the representational mandala which is depicted with colors, hand gestures, and so forth. CE. See also **Vajrayana**.

ngondro [Tib. *sngo 'gro*]. Literally, "before going," the term *Ngondro* refers to the set of four or five "extraordinary" preliminary practices that prepare the heart and mind of a practitioner to receive and engage in the profound inner practices of Tibetan Buddhism. A practitioner begins by contemplating the four thoughts that turn the mind from samsara, known as the "common ngondro." Afterwards, he or she engages in the five aspects of "extraordinary Ngondro" or "inner Ngondro," which include (1) taking refuge with prostrations, (2) cultivating bodhichitta, (3) making mandala offerings, (4) meditating on Vajrasattva, and (5) engaging in Guru

Yoga. Each of these practices should be completed 100,000 times.

nine yanas [Tib. *theg pa dgu*]. According to the Nyingma school of Tibetan Buddhism, the 84,000 teachings of the Buddha can all be summarized in terms of the nine yanas [*thegpa*], or "vehicles." They are:

(1) Shravakayana, or "Hearer Vehicle"
(2) Pratyekabuddhayana, or "Solitary Realizer Vehicle"
(3) Bodhisattvayana, or "Bodhisattva Vehicle"
(4) Kriyayogatantra, or "Action Yoga Tantra"
(5) Upayogatantra, or "Dual Yoga Tantra"
(6) Yogayogatantra, or "Yoga Tantra"
(7) Mahayogatantra, or "Great Yoga Tantra"
(8) Anuyogatantra, or "Subsequent Yoga Tantra"
(9) Atiyogatantra, or "Supreme Yoga Tantra"

According to the Nyingma classification, the first two yanas are known as "Foundational Buddhism," or "Hinayana," and all the rest of the yanas—from the third through the ninth—are known as "Mahayana." The Vajrayana, also known as "Tantrayana," includes everything from Kriyayoga (the fourth yana) up to and including Atiyoga (the ninth). Yanas four through six—Kriyayoga, Upayoga, and Yogayoga—comprise the Outer Tantras, while yanas seven through nine—Mahayoga, Anuyoga, and Atiyoga—make up the Inner Tantras. PONM, CE. See also **Dzogchen, Hinayana, Mahayana,** and **Vajrayana.**

nirmanakaya [Skt.; Tib. *sprul sku*]. Literally, "buddha body of emanation," *nirmanakaya* is the union of the empty (dharmakaya) and luminous (sambhogakaya) aspects of awareness, or reality, which manifests as an unceasing display of wisdom, compassion, and loving-kindness. The term *nirmanakaya* can also refer to the physical emanation of enlightened beings that arises spontaneously and inseparably from the dharmakaya and sambhogakaya. CE. See also **dharmakaya** and **sambhogakaya**.

nirvana [Skt.; Tib. *myang 'das*]. This term is used in various ways in the different levels of Buddhist teaching. Literally, "the state beyond sorrow," *nirvana* generally indicates the realization in which all afflictive mental states that misapprehend reality as it is and thus perpetuate suffering are completely and permanently uprooted. In classical Buddhist literature, there are three types of nirvana: (1) with residue, in which a person is still dependent upon the karmically conditioned aggregates; (2) without residue, in which the aggregates "have been consumed within emptiness"; and (3) nonabiding nirvana that is free from the extremes of quiescence and cyclic existence. The achievement of the transcendental wisdom rainbow body corresponds to the highest level of enlightenment. HEC, SPG, TBD.

Noble Eightfold Path [Tib. *'phags lam gyi yan lag brgyad*]. The Noble Eightfold Path is the fourth of the Four Noble Truths [*bden pa rnam bzhi*] taught by the Buddha, which include the truths of (1) suffering, (2) the cause of suffering, (3) cessation, and (4) the path that leads to cessation. The Noble Eightfold Path is divided into (1) right view, (2) right intention, (3) right speech, (4) right conduct, (5) right livelihood, (6) right effort, (7) right mindfulness, and (8) right concentration. SPG, CE. See also **Four Noble Truths**.

Nyingma [Tib. *rnying ma*]. Also the "Old Translation" or "Early Dissemination" school of Tibetan Buddhism, Nyingma refers to the teachings that were brought to Tibet during the eighth to ninth centuries and translated mostly by Padmasambhava, Vimalamitra, Shantarakshita, and Vairochana during the reign of Dharma King Trisong Deutsen. Up until the time of Rinchen Zangpo, in the 9th century, Buddhism flourished in the Land of Snows. At that point, the evil Langdarma persecuted the Dharma and its practitioners to such an extent that it only survived in Tibet due to the blessings of the great lineage masters and the diligence of lay practitioners who secretly upheld and preserved the teachings. The so-called "new schools" [Tib. *Sarma*] of Tibetan Buddhism—the Gelug-Kadam, Sakya, and Kagyu traditions—are based primarily on "new translations" of the Dharma that were undertaken after the end of this religious persecution, when a new wave of Buddhist teachings were introduced from India during the eleventh century. It was after this point that the early dissemination of Buddhism in Tibet came to be known as "Nyingma," or "Ancient Translation school."

The Nyingma school is transmitted in two forms: the long lineage of kama and the short lineage of terma. Additionally, Nyingmapas classify the Buddhist teachings into nine vehicles, which are based on the capacity of individual students. These vehicles are subdivided into three causal vehicles and six resultant vehicles. The causal vehicles include (1) the Hearer Vehicle (Shravakayana), the (2) Solitary Realizer Vehicle (Pratyekabuddhayana), and (3) the Bodhisattva Vehicle (Bodhisattvayana). The resultant vehicles of the Vajrayana include the lower tantras and the higher tantras: (4) Kriyatantra, (5) Upatantra, (6) Yogatantra, and (7) Mahayoga, (8) Anuyoga, and (9) Atiyoga, respectively. Generally speaking, Nyingmapas emphasize the three higher tantras, with Dzogchen (Atiyoga) being the pinnacle of all vehicles. LFIW, NSTB, SPG, WN. See also **Dzogchen** and **nine yanas**.

prajna. See **wisdom**.

rigpa [Tib. *rig pa*]. The general Buddhist teachings use the Tibetan term *rigpa* to indicate (1) conceptual knowledge or understanding, whereas the Dzogchen teachings use it to indicate (2) intrinsic awareness, which is non-conceptual wisdom. As the Venerable

Rinpoches explain in *Tara's Enlightened Activity* (Snow Lion, 2007),

> Rigpa has the three characteristics of [1] emptiness, [2] clarity, and [3] unceasing energy. The emptiness aspect of rigpa is dharmakaya; the clarity—or brightness aspect—of rigpa is sambhogakaya; and the unceasing compassionate energy of rigpa is nirmanakaya. Tara has the "endowment" of these three natural states. We could use the word "settling" for her condition of endowment. When we recognize this rigpa and relax or settle into it, we instantly just settle in the dharmakaya state. We don't have to move anywhere and we don't have to transfer ourselves from one state to another. All dualistic conceptions dissolve, or self-liberate, just as ice melts into water. The chunks of ice are our habitual patterns and...[the obstacles we experience] are our dualistic creations. Now, all that melts into the original state and we reach enlightenment in the embodiment of the three kayas. This is the supreme realization, the quick realization, and the highest teaching. We practitioners are fortunate to have become connected to the Dzogchen teachings (173).

samadhi [Skt.; Tib. *ting nge 'dzin*]. Rangjung Yeshe defines *samadhi* as "adhering to the continuity of evenness, a state of undistracted concentration or meditative absorption which in the context of Vajrayana can refer to either the development stage or the completion stage." Samadhi is one of the themes of the paramitas and the Noble Eightfold Path taught by Buddha Shakyamuni. In fact, the Noble Eightfold Path can be divided into teachings belonging to three categories: (1) *shila* [*tshul khrims*], ethical conduct; (2) *samadhi*, concentration associated with meditative equipoise; and (3) *prajna* [*shes rab*], transcendent wisdom. Jamgon Kongtrul the Great defines the Tibetan word *tingedzin* in several ways: "concentration, mental focus, meditative stabilization, meditative absorption, contemplation, state of contemplation, absorption, total involvement, undividedness, deep concentration," etc. The word *samadhi* can also refer to one of the "seven causes of enlightenment" or to the "three samadhis" [*ting nge 'dzin rnam pa gsum*] of the Vajrayana associated with the creation and completion stages. The latter include (1) the "suchness samadhi" [*de bzhin nyid kyi ting nge 'dzin*], (2) the "all-illuminating samadhi" [*kun tu snang ba'i ting nge 'dzin*], and (3) the "seed (syllable) samadhi" [*rgyu yi ting nge 'dzin*]. CE, OWDOT, RYG; Leigh Brasington, "Sharpening Manjushri's Sword: The Jhanas in Theravadan Buddhist Meditation," 1997, <http://www.leighb.com/jhana2.htm>, retrieved February 2011. See also **Shamatha**.

samaya [Skt.; Tib. *dam tshig*]. The Tibetan word *damtsig* literally means "promise," "agreement," or "engagement." In order to maintain a pure connection with one's Vajra Guru and vajra brothers and sisters, it is very important to uphold one's samayas with them. Mipham Rinpoche discusses the general meaning of this term in *Luminous Essence* (Snow Lion, 2009):

> [S]amaya … means something that is not to be transgressed. It also refers to the commands of great beings. Samayas are points of training that masterful practitioners do not transgress, but enact in accordance with what is to be engaged in and rejected…. In brief, the mantra samayas are condensed into three categories: [1] the general samayas, [2] particular samayas, and [3] superior samayas. General samayas are explained to be the vows of individual liberation [Hinayana], the trainings of the awakened mind [bodhichitta or Bodhisattvayana], and the samayas of outer mantra. Since these are not to be transgressed, without any real purpose, they form the foundation for, and are a facet of, the samayas of unsurpassable mantra. For this reason, they are also called the "common general samayas." The particular samayas are said to be the root and branch samayas that are found throughout the unsurpassable mantra itself.

sambhogakaya [Skt.; Tib. *longs spyod rdzogs pa'i sku*]. Literally, the "buddha body of complete enjoyment," *sambhogakaya* is the energy, clarity, and vitality of one's own innate awareness, or dharmakaya; it is the spontaneously accomplished and inherent richness of wisdom. From the emptiness of the dharmakaya, the sambhogakaya manifests at a very subtle level and is usually perceived only by those with a very high degree of realization. Although one can speak of the three kayas as separate things, they are ultimately indivisible. HEC. See also **dharmakaya** and **nirmanakaya**.

samsara [Skt.; Tib. *khor wa*]. *Samsara* is conditioned by fundamental ignorance, afflictive mental states, and *karma*. These arise in conjunction with the twelve links of interdependent origination. Sentient beings take birth somewhere in the six realms and inevitably experience old age, sickness, death, and rebirth. Fundamentally, samsara does not exist outside of mind, since it is nothing other than delusion—the failure to recognize the nature of reality as it is. From this perspective, not recognizing the true nature is samsara, while recognizing the true nature is nirvana. DIF. See also **karma**, **nirvana**, **six realms**, and **twelve links of interdependent causation**.

samten. See **Shamatha**.

sangha [Skt.; Tib. *dge 'dun*]. The *sangha* is the third of the Three Jewels in which a practitioner takes refuge. Broadly speaking, this term refers to students of the Dharma or spiritual friends of four types: (1) monks, (2) nuns, (3) lay male practitioners, and (4) lay female practitioners. Specifically, the "noble sangha" is comprised of those who have achieved the first bhumi (the path of seeing) and beyond. GI. See also **buddha**, **Dharma**, and **Three Jewels**.

Shamatha [Skt.; Tib. *zhi gnas*]. Type of meditation in which the mind remains focused on an object of concentration. One can practice Shamatha with focus or Shamatha without focus. In either case, there is a very subtle idea present that meditation is taking place, which is different from maintaining awareness of rigpa; i.e. there is a meditator, a meditative technique, and the act of meditation. Shamatha meditation is indispensable for concentrating the mind so that insight [Skt. *Vipashyana*], or lucid, transparent awareness of the arising, abiding, and ceasing of phenomena can be applied. Dzogchen is the union of absolute Shamatha and absolute Vipashyana. See also **samadhi** and **Vipashyana**.

sherab. See **wisdom**.

shila [Skt.; Tib. *tshul khrims*]. The Sanskrit word *shila* means "to make correct," "to behave ethically," or "to discipline oneself." To train in discipline means we choose our direction according to right and wrong, abandoning wild and negative actions in favor of gentle and positive ones. In the practice of the second paramita, we discipline the total expression of our body, speech, and mind. The three categories of discipline include (1) discipline that rejects negative actions, (2) discipline that accepts positive actions, and (3) discipline that benefits all sentient beings. CE. See also **concentration, six paramitas, three trainings**, and **wisdom**.

six paramitas [Tib. *pha rol tu phyin pa drug*; Skt. *satparamita*]. The "six perfections" are a bridge we use to cross from samsara's shore of delusion to the other shore of enlightenment, and are thus the principal practices of the bodhisattvas. They are (1) generosity, (2) self-discipline, (3) patience, (4) joyful effort, (5) concentration, and (6) wisdom. We usually do our practice on a cushion, maintaining the mind in its natural state, which is free from concepts. This is the combined practice of the fifth paramita of concentration and the sixth paramita of wisdom, or emptiness meditation. But it is difficult to maintain this kind of practice when engaged in normal, everyday activities. So, in order to help bodhisattvas carry their Dharma practice out into the world to benefit others, the Buddha taught the first three paramitas of generosity, self-discipline, and patience. These are methods of training in actual post-meditation activities rooted in loving-kindness and compassion. The fourth paramita of joyful effort is considered to be an essential support of all the other paramitas, whether related with meditation or post-meditation. CE. See also **bodhisattva**, **concentration**, **shila**, and **wisdom**.

six realms [Tib. *rigs drug gi gnas*; Skt. *satgati*]. The six realms are named according to the six classes of beings who inhabit them: (1) gods [*lha*], (2) *asuras* [*lha min*], (3) human beings [*mi*], (4) animals [*dud 'grol*], (5) hungry ghosts [*yi dvags*], and (6) hell beings [*dmyal ba*]. These realms are caused and dominated by particular mental poisons: arrogance, jealousy, desire, bewilderment or ignorance, miserliness, and anger, respectively. The "three higher realms" are the god, asura, and human realms, whereas the "three lower realms" are the animal, hungry ghost, and hell realms. In the Buddhist teachings, it is often explained that humans inhabit the most favorable realm for spiritual practice. The god realms are so blissful that beings reborn there waste their time enjoying various pleasures; the asuras or demigods are always fighting and jealously scheming on how to overcome the gods; the animal realms are plagued by ignorance, and animals are subject to the whims of others, busy eating and being eaten by each other; hungry ghosts are tormented by a constant lack of food and water; and the hell realms are so painful and filled with agony that hell beings cannot easily cultivate bodhichitta or virtuous mental states. In contrast, the human realm has a relatively full spectrum of experience— enough pain and suffering that humans want to find a way out of it, and enough pleasure that they are attached to being human. Humans can willingly and deliberately cultivate the mental states and activities that lead to positive rebirths. Additionally, the human mind and physical structures are such that they can understand the teachings and put them into practice, eventually achieving enlightenment. CE. See also **karma** and **samsara**.

Sutras [Skt.; Tib. *mdo, mdo sde*]. One of the Three Baskets (*Tripitaka*), the others being the *Vinaya* and the *Abhidharma*. They are original discourses given by Buddha Shakyamuni to his disciples. A *sutra* always begins with the statement, "Thus I have heard," followed by details of the time and place at which the sutra was taught, the students' questions and the Buddha's answers, and concluding with everyone rejoicing in the teachings. These discourses were compiled and transcribed by his arhat followers during the "First Council" held shortly after the Awakened One's *mahaparinirvana*, especially with the help of his cousin and long-time attendant Ananda [*kun dga'*], who possessed the siddhi of perfect recall, as well as arhats Mahakashyapa [*'od srung chen po*] and Upali [*nye bar 'khor*]. The sutras are classified as belonging either to the Hinayana or Mahayana, depending on whether they are related with the first, second, or third turnings of the wheel of Dharma. CE, DIF. See also **Abhidharma**, **Hinayana**, **Mahayana**, **Three Baskets**, and **Vinaya**.

tantra [Skt.; Tib. *rgyud*]. The Sanskrit word *tantra* literally means "continuity" or "continuum." As the Venerable Rinpoches explain in SPG, "[W]hat is continuing? In the context of the *Guhyagarbha Tantra*, the profound and beautiful qualities of the inherent richness nature of each and every being are continuing. This nature continues without any interruption whatsoever, regardless of the external changes we go through related with circumstances and situations. External changes never affect the continuity of the reality nature we all share." And as the Rangjung Yeshe Wiki explains, "[*Tantra* refers to] the Vajrayana teachings given by the Buddha in his sambhogakaya form. The real sense of tantra is 'continuity', the innate buddha nature, which is known as the 'tantra of the expressed meaning.' The general sense of tantra is the extraordinary tantric scriptures also known as the 'tantra of the expressing words.' Can also refer to all the resultant teachings of Vajrayana as a whole." Finally, *tantra* is often discussed in the context of "ground tantra," "path tantra," and "fruition tantra." RYW, SPG. See also **Vajrayana**.

tathagatagarbha [Skt.; Tib. *de bzhin gshegs pa'i snying po*]. Literally, the "essence of the tathagatas" and a synonym for "buddha-nature." The Venerable Rinpoches explain the meaning of the Sanskrit word *tathata* in OWDRS:

> [W]hen we say "true nature," what exactly does this refer to? It refers to "suchness," or *debzhin nyid* [*de bzhin nyid*] in Tibetan. This is known as *tathata* in Sanskrit. I have also seen this term translated as "thatness" and "thusness"... [W]hat is this true nature? It is the original nature of great emptiness, which is pure from the beginning and inseparable from clarity. Regarding suchness, there is no difference between sentient beings and buddhas—all are the same. This is why the Buddha said, "Regardless of whether or not a buddha appears in the world and gives teachings, the nature is always unchanging. Had a buddha not appeared and taught in this world, the nature would not have changed in any way. The nature is always the same." So, there is no difference between the nature of a buddha and the nature of sentient beings. For this reason, regular sentient beings can reach enlightenment. OWDRS.

ten virtuous actions [Tib. *so nam, ge we le*; Skt. *kushala*]. The virtuous activities of body, speech, and mind reflect and strengthen one's bodhichitta, and therefore lead to positive results. The three virtues of body are (1) saving and prolonging life, (2) being generous, and (3) maintaining moral conduct. The four virtues of speech are speaking (4) gently, (5) honestly, (6) harmoniously, and (7) meaningfully. The three virtues of mind are (8) contentment, (9) loving-kindness, and (10) right view. The opposite of these are the ten non-virtuous actions, which include: (1) killing, (2) stealing, (3) sexual misconduct, (4) abusive words, (5) lying, (6) slander, (7) idle gossip, (8) covetousness, (9) ill-will, and (10) wrong views. DIF. See also **shila** and **six paramitas**.

Theravada. See **Hinayana**.

Three Baskets. The Sanskrit term *Tripitaka* literally means "three baskets," referring to the Vinaya, Sutra, and Abhidharma teachings of Buddha Shakyamuni. CE. See also **Abhidharma, Sutras,** and **Vinaya**.

Three Jewels [Tib. *dkon mchog gsum*; Skt. *triratna*]. Referring to the Buddha, Dharma, and Sangha, a Buddhist practitioner takes refuge in the "Three Jewels," which offer protection from the endless sufferings and confusion of samsara. Although in this case "Buddha" refers to the historical Buddha Shakyamuni, on a more subtle level the Buddha represents the nature of reality, the nature of the five kayas and five wisdoms. The "Dharma" is the teachings, the words, names, and letters used to convey the holy instructions of the Noble Ones. And the "Sangha," or community of practitioners, includes the *actual* sangha of realized beings— those who have minimally achieved the path of seeing—and the *resembling* sangha of practitioners still on the path of accumulation or joining. His Holiness Dudjom Rinpoche explains the inner meaning of the Three Jewels:

> Externally, the Buddha is the guide, the source of Dharma; the Dharma is the path that Buddha showed; and the Sangha members

are the people whose minds are turned toward the Dharma. The Buddha, Dharma, and Sangha also exist internally and symbolically as a profound and skillful way to lead us out of samsara. From the point of view of absolute truth, even the Buddha, Dharma, and Sangha are within us. Our mind is empty, radiant and aware, and that is the precious Buddha. Externally, the Dharma manifests as words and meaning that are heard and practiced, but internally the Dharma is the empty, unobstructed and self-luminous display of *rigpa*, or nondual awareness. Externally, the followers of the Dharma are the Sangha, but internally the Sangha is the all-pervading, all-encompassing quality of the mind. The three jewels are inherent within us, but since we do not recognize this, we take refuge externally in the Buddha, Dharma, and Sangha with devotion.

What actually distinguishes Buddhists from non-Buddhists is taking refuge in the Three Jewels. IP. See also **buddha**, **Dharma**, **ngondro**, and **sangha**.

three kayas. See **dharmakaya**, **sambhogakaya**, and **nirmanakaya**.

three trainings [Tib. *lhag pa'i bslab pa gsum*]. The Noble Eightfold Path can be divided into teachings belonging to three categories: (1) *shila* [Skt.; Tib. *tshul khrims*], ethical conduct; (2) *samadhi* [Skt.; Tib. *ting nge 'dzin*], concentration associated with meditative equipoise; and (3) *prajna* [Skt.; Tib. *shes rab*], transcendent wisdom. EJLD, Vol. 1. See also **concentration**, **Noble Eightfold Path**, **shila**, and **wisdom**.

three yanas. See **Hinayana**, **Mahayana**, and **Vajrayana**.

three wisdoms. See **wisdom**.

tsultrim. See **shila**.

twelve links of interdependent causation [Tib. *rten cing 'brel bar 'byung ba'i tshul bcu gnyis*; Skt. *Dvadashangapratityasamutpada*]. Often translated into English as "dependent origination," "dependent arising," or "interdependent coordination," it is commonly taught that Buddha Shakyamuni awoke to complete enlightenment by understanding the profound nature of the interdependence of all phenomena. The twelve links of dependent origination [Skt. *nidanas*], which were taught in the Abhidharma discourses of the first turning of the wheel of Dharma, demonstrate the process through which all phenomena arise interdependently based on karma, causes, and conditions. These links are traditionally ordered as follows: (1) ignorance, (2) karmic formations or habitual tendencies, (3) dualistic consciousness, (4) name and form, (5) the six sense organs—or fields—of the eye, ear, nose, tongue, body, and dualistic consciousness, (6) contact, (7) feeling or physical sensation, (8) thirst or craving, (9) grasping, (10) becoming or being, (11) birth, and (12) old age and death. The entire process is driven by ignorance, defined by the mahapandita Mipham Jamyang Namgyal Gyatso as "not knowing the Four Noble Truths and assuming that the ongoing movement of the five aggregates is an enduring 'self.'" IT, NSTB.

two truths [Tib. *bden pa gnyis*; Skt. *satya dvaya*]. The two truths include relative truth [*kun rdzob kyi bden pa*] and absolute truth [*don dam bden pa*]. Taught by Buddha Shakyamuni principally during the second and third turnings of the Wheel of Dharma, the teachings on absolute truth emphasize the nature of all phenomena, or emptiness, whereas teachings on relative truth emphasize the manifest, radiating qualities of the nature, including the inherent, beautiful qualities of buddha-nature. In general, relative truth describes that which accords with conventional, worldly understanding of phenomena; however, when subjected to thorough analysis, the solidity of phenomena dissolves. All phenomena are thus revealed to be dependently arisen mere appearances with the nature of emptiness. CE, LDWD.

Vajrayana [Skt.; Tib. *rdo rje'i theg pa*]. The Vajrayana is also known as the "Adamantine Vehicle," "Indestructible Vehicle," "Secret Mantrayana" [*gsang ngags kyi theg pa*; Skt. *Guhyamantra*], and "Mantrayana." The latter two names indicate that mind is protected from dualistic conceptions through the practice of this vehicle. In the Sanskrit word *mantra*, the root *mana* can be translated as "mind" and the suffix *tra* can be translated as "protection." On one level, the Vajrayana is referred to as "secret" because it has traditionally been transmitted from a qualified teacher to a qualified disciple and kept hidden from those who would misinterpret the teachings and thereby harm themselves and others. However, on a deeper level, this secret quality alludes to the "self-secret" nature of awareness that remains hidden from duality mind. There are two very important foundational elements to all Vajrayana practice: (1) a vast and sincere motivation of bodhichitta, which is the strong wish to bring all sentient beings, without partiality, to the state of complete enlightenment, and (2) a purity understanding or view of the nature, which regards all phenomena—including one's own aggregates—as the pervasive wisdom display of the "three vajra states" [*rdo rje gsum*], the inseparable union of wisdom and compassion.

Within this context, the Vajrayana is characterized by innumerable tantric techniques, such as visualization, mantra recitation, and various yogic disciplines, all of which are designed to bring every aspect of experience—including the eight consciousnesses, all mental events, the five poisons, and the six bardos—to the path of Dharma. This is ultimately accomplished by stabilizing recognition of the nature of mind, which is the primordial union of appearance and emptiness, or wisdom and compassion. In general, the Vajrayana (Buddhist tantra) is said to have ten characteristics, listed by Namkhai Norbu Rinpoche as follows: (1) outlook [view], (2) meditation, (3) behavior [conduct], (4) initiation [empowerment], (5) mandala, (6) charismatic activity, (7) commitments [samayas], (8) capacities, (9) worship, and (10) mantra. These diverse methods utilize the dynamic power of mental, physical, and verbal activities to transcend and transform mundane habit patterns into their corresponding wisdom nature. For instance, the five poisons are ultimately experienced as the five wisdoms. Through the skillful means of the Vajrayana, a practitioner uses the previously overwhelming power of the negativities and defilements to connect with the primordial purity of both awareness and phenomena, of subject, object, and action.

The Nyingma school divides the Vajrayana teachings into three Outer Tantras (Kriyatantra, Upatantra, and Yogatantra) and three Inner Tantras (Mahayoga, Anuyoga, and Atiyoga). In contrast with the "causal" teachings of the Sutrayana, the Vajrayana teachings are known as "resultant" because "the indestructible and imperishable realities of buddha-body, speech, and mind are fully realized and manifested when the continuum of the ground is transformed into the continuum of the result by means of the continuum of the path." In other words, when the *alaya* [*kun gzhi*, i.e., the ground] is purified of dualistic conceptions, karmic imprints, and obscurations by practicing on all forms, sounds, and thoughts as the wisdom display of awareness through the various techniques of the Secret Mantra (i.e., path), body, speech, and mind are realized and manifest as the displays of enlightenment, none other than the shining qualities of one's own innate nature (i.e., result). Hence, the ground and result are essentially identical: the *ground* is primordial awareness, the inherent, original nature of tantra that is the indestructible, unborn true nature; and the *result* is complete recognition and understanding of this nature as an unbroken, vivid experience that transcends the duality of subject, object, and action. This true nature of reality—primordial, nondual awareness, or the innermost nature of mind itself—is known as *rigpa* in Dzogchen terminology. OWDOT, SPG, RYG, TBD; Longchenpa, *You Are the Eyes of the World*, trans. by Kennard Lipman and Merrill Peterson (Ithaca: Snow Lion Publications, 2000). See also **tantra**.

Vinaya [Skt.; Tib. *'dul ba*]. As the first of the Three Baskets, the *Vinaya* includes the Buddha's teachings on ethics in general, and on monastic discipline in particular. The Vinaya is founded on the Pratimoksha vows. PONM. See also **Abhidharma**, **Hinayana**, **shila**, **Sutras**, and **Three Baskets**.

Vipashyana [Skt.; Tib. *lhag mthong*]. In general, this is known as insight meditation, or the open quality of awareness which penetrates the nature of its selected object. On the ultimate level, Vipashyana refers to resting in the transparent, lucid state of the true nature, free from conceptual thoughts or elaboration. After having developed one-pointed concentration through Shamatha meditation, one infuses that concentration with penetrating insight into the nature of reality. Dzogchen is the union of absolute Shamatha and absolute Vipashyana. See also **Shamatha**.

visualization stage. See **creation stage**.

wisdom [Tib. *shes rab*; Skt. *pra jna*]. In the Sanskrit word *prajna*, the word *pra* means "supreme," "primordial," or "pure," and *jna* means "wisdom." Supreme, transcendental wisdom is the antidote to all dualistic thinking, which is rooted in ignorance. When we train in the sixth paramita, we are developing the ability to see with clear, open, unmistaken, and undistorted vision. We will gradually gain an understanding of the true nature of reality in both its relative and absolute aspects. The three categories of wisdom are called *thopa* [*thos pa*], *sampa* [*bsam pa*], and *gompa* [*sgom pa*]. They refer to the wisdoms that come from (1) hearing, or study; (2) contemplation, or understanding; and (3) meditation, or total integration. CE. See also **Dzogchen**, **six paramitas**, and **two truths**.

yana [Tib. *theg pa*]. See **nine yanas**.

LIST OF FIGURES

All gonpa wall and mural photographs are used with permission. © Padmasambhava Buddhist Center

Venerable Khenpo Rinpoches

ABOUT THE AUTHORS

VEN. KHENCHEN PALDEN SHERAB RINPOCHE (1938-2010)

Venerable Khenchen Palden Sherab Rinpoche was a renowned scholar and meditation master of the Nyingma school of Tibetan Buddhism. He was born on May 10, 1938 in the Doshul region of Kham in eastern Tibet, near the sacred mountain Jowo Zegyal. On the morning of his birth, a small snow fell with flakes in the shape of lotus petals. Among his ancestors were many great scholars, practitioners, and tertons.

His family was semi-nomadic, living in the village during the winter and moving with the herds to high mountain pastures in the summer, where they lived in yak hair tents. The monastery for the Doshul region is known as Gochen Monastery, founded by the great terton Tsasum Lingpa, and his father's family had the hereditary responsibility for administration of the business affairs of the monastery. His grandfather had been both administrator and chantmaster in charge of the ritual ceremonies.

Khenchen Rinpoche began his education at Gochen Monastery at age four. He entered Riwoche Monastery at age fourteen, completing his studies there just before the Chinese invasion of Tibet reached the area. Among his root teachers was the illustrious Khenchen Tenzin Dragpa (Katok Khenpo Ashe).

In 1959, Khenchen Rinpoche and his family were forced into exile, escaping to India. After the tumultuous period following their escape, in 1967 he was appointed head of the Nyingma department of the Central Institute of Higher Tibetan Studies in Sarnath by His Holiness Dudjom Rinpoche, the Supreme Head of the Nyingma school of Tibetan Buddhism. He held this position of abbot for seventeen years, dedicating all his time and energy to ensure the survival and spread of the Buddha's teachings.

Venerable Khenchen Palden Sherab Rinpoche moved to the United States in 1984 to work closely with His Holiness Dudjom Rinpoche. In 1985, he and his brother, Venerable Khenpo Tsewang Dongyal Rinpoche, founded the Dharma Samudra Publishing Company. In 1988, they founded the Padmasambhava Buddhist Center (PBC), which has centers throughout the United States, as well as Puerto Rico, Russia, and India, among others. The principal center is Palden Padma Samye Ling, located in Delaware County, upstate New York. PBC also includes a traditional Tibetan Buddhist monastery and nunnery at the holy site of Deer Park in Sarnath, and the Miracle Stupa for World Peace at Padma Samye Jetavan, which is in Jetavan Grove in Shravasti, India.

Khenchen Palden Sherab Rinpoche traveled extensively within the United States and throughout the world, giving teachings and empowerments, conducting retreats and seminars, and establishing meditation centers. He authored three volumes of Tibetan works, and co-authored over thirty books in English with Venerable Khenpo Tsewang Dongyal Rinpoche. His collected Tibetan works include:

Advice from the Ancestral Vidyadhara, a commentary on Padmasambhava's *Stages of the Path, Heap of Jewels*

Blazing Clouds of Wisdom and Compassion, a commentary on the hundred-syllable mantra of Vajrasattva

Clouds of Blessings, an explanation of prayers to Terchen Tsasum Lingpa, and other learned works, poems, prayers and sadhanas

The Essence of Diamond Clear Light, an outline and structural analysis of *The Aspiration Prayer of Samantabhadra*

The Mirror of Mindfulness, an explanation of the six bardos

Opening the Eyes of Wisdom, a commentary on Sangye Yeshe's *Lamp of the Eye of Contemplation*

Opening the Door of Blessings, a biography of Machig Labdron

The Ornament of Stars at Dawn, an outline and structural analysis of Vasubandhu's *Twenty Verses*

The Ornament of Vairochana's Intention, a commentary on the *Heart Sutra*

Lotus Necklace of Devotion, a biography of Khenchen Tenzin Dragpa

Pleasure Lake of Nagarjuna's Intention, a general summary of Madhyamaka

The Radiant Light of the Sun and Moon, a commentary on Mipham Rinpoche's *The Sword of Wisdom That Ascertains Reality*

The Smile of Sun and Moon: A Commentary on the Praise to the Twenty-One Taras

Smiling Red Lotus, a short commentary on the prayer to Yeshe Tsogyal

Supreme Clear Mirror, an introduction to Buddhist logic

Waves of the Ocean of Devotion, a biography-praise to Nubchen Sangye Yeshe, and Vajra Rosary, biographies of his main incarnations

White Lotus, an explanation of prayers to Guru Rinpoche

VEN. KHENPO TSEWANG DONGYAL RINPOCHE

Venerable Khenpo Tsewang Dongyal Rinpoche was born in the Doshul region of Kham in eastern Tibet, on June 10, 1950. On that summer day in the family tent, Khenpo Rinpoche's birth caused his mother Pema Lhadze no pain. The next day, upon moving the bed where she had delivered the baby, his mother found growing a beautiful and fragrant flower, which she  plucked and offered to Chenrezig on the family altar.

Soon after Khenpo Tsewang was born, three head lamas from Jadchag Monastery came to his home and recognized him as the reincarnation of Khenpo Sherab Khyentse, who had been the former head abbot at Gochen Monastery. Sherab Khyentse was a renowned scholar and practitioner who spent much of his life in retreat.

Khenpo Rinpoche began his formal schooling at age five when he entered Gochen Monastery. However, his first Dharma teacher was his father, Lama Chimed Namgyal Rinpoche. The Chinese invasion of Tibet interrupted his studies, and he escaped to India with his family in 1959. There his father and brother continued his education until he entered the Nyingmapa Monastic School of northern India, where he studied until 1967. Khenpo Rinpoche then entered the Central Institute of Higher Tibetan Studies, which at the time was part of Sanskrit University in Varanasi, where he received his BA degree in 1975. He also attended Nyingmapa University in West Bengal, where he received another BA and an MA in 1977.

In 1978, His Holiness Dudjom Rinpoche enthroned Venerable Khenpo Tsewang Dongyal Rinpoche as the abbot of the Wish-fulfilling Nyingmapa Institute in Boudanath, Nepal, where he taught poetry, grammar, and philosophy. Then, in 1981, His Holiness appointed Khenpo Rinpoche as the abbot of the Dorje Nyingpo center in Paris, France. Finally, in 1982, he asked Khenpo Tsewang to work with him at the Yeshe Nyingpo center in New York. From that time until His Holiness Dudjom Rinpoche's mahaparinirvana in 1987, Khenpo Rinpoche continued to work closely with him, often traveling with His Holiness as his translator and attendant.

In 1988, Khenpo Tsewang Dongyal Rinpoche and his brother, Venerable Khenchen Palden Sherab Rinpoche, founded the Padmasambhava Buddhist Center. Since that time, he has served as a spiritual director at the various Padmasambhava Buddhist centers throughout the world. He maintains an active traveling and teaching schedule. Khenpo Rinpoche is the author of *Light of Fearless Indestructible Wisdom: The Life and Legacy of His Holiness Dudjom Rinpoche*, published in both Tibetan and English. He has also authored a book of poetry on the life of Guru Rinpoche entitled *Praise to the Lotus Born: A Verse Garland of Waves of Devotion*, and a unique two-volume cultural and religious history of Tibet entitled *Six Sublime Pillars of the Nyingma School*, which details the historical bases of the Dharma in Tibet from the 6th to 9th centuries. At present, *Six Sublime Pillars* is one of the only books to convey the Dharma activities of this period in such depth, and His Holiness Dudjom Rinpoche encouraged Khenpo Tsewang to complete it, describing the work as an important contribution to the history of the Kama lineage.

Along with these, Khenpo Tsewang Dongyal Rinpoche has co-authored over thirty Dharma books in English with Venerable Khenchen Palden Sherab Rinpoche.

PADMA SAMYE LING SHEDRA SERIES

The Venerable Khenpo Rinpoches have taught the Dharma in the United States for more than thirty years. In that time, they have given over a decade of shedra teachings. These clear and profound teachings include detailed summaries and commentaries by great Nyingma masters such as Kunkhyen Longchenpa and Mipham Rinpoche. Each of the PSL Shedra Series books distills the essential meaning of the Nyingma Shedra program that the Venerable Rinpoches received in Tibet as the last generation of lamas to be taught in the traditional monastic setting, which had carefully preserved the lineage teachings for centuries.

The PSL Shedra Series is developing into a complete and comprehensive Nyingma shedra curriculum that will serve as the basis for the present and future study of the Buddhadharma in PBC centers. It is our hope that these books will provide a solid framework for traditional Tibetan Buddhist study by people in the English-speaking world, whose busy lives do not easily allow for more extended periods of retreat and study.

With the PSL Shedra Series, the Venerable Khenpo Rinpoches are directly sustaining and glorifying the study curriculum that has enabled the Buddhadharma to be successfully carried from generation to generation. By developing intelligent, thorough analysis, practitioners establish a reliable foundation for realizing the path of enlightenment. The PSL Shedra Series currently includes:

(Nine Yanas) *Turning the Wisdom Wheel of the Nine Golden Chariots*

(Vol. 1)   *Opening the Clear Vision of the Vaibhashika and Sautrantika Schools*

(Vol. 2)   *Opening the Clear Vision of the Mind Only School*

OTHER PUBLICATIONS
BY THE VENERABLE KHENPO RINPOCHES

Advice from a Spiritual Friend: A Commentary on Nagarjuna's Letter to a Friend

The Beauty of Awakened Mind: Dzogchen Lineage of the Great Master Shigpo Dudtsi

The Buddhist Path: A Practical Guide from the Nyingma Tradition of Tibetan Buddhism (formerly titled *Opening to Our Primordial Nature*)

Ceaseless Echoes of the Great Silence: A Commentary on the Heart Sutra (English and Spanish)

Cutting Through Ego and Revealing Fearlessness: Chod Practice According to Jigme Lingpa's Bellowing Laugh of the Dakini

The Dark Red Amulet: Oral Instructions on the Practice of Vajrakilaya

Discovering Infinite Freedom: The Prayer of Kuntuzangpo

Door to Inconceivable Wisdom and Compassion

The Essential Journey of Life and Death
    Volume I: Indestructible Nature of Body, Speech, and Mind
    Volume II: Using Dream Yoga and Phowa as the Path

Heart Essence of Chetsun: Voice of the Lion (restricted)

Illuminating the Path: Ngondro Instructions According to the Nyingma School of Vajrayana Buddhism (English and Spanish)

Walking in the Footsteps of the Buddha

Inborn Realization: A Commentary on His Holiness Dudjom Rinpoche's Mountain Retreat Instructions

Liberating Duality with Wisdom Display: The Eight Manifestations of Guru Padmasambhava

Light of Fearless Indestructible Wisdom: The Life and Legacy of His Holiness Dudjom Rinpoche

Light of Peace: How Buddhism Shines in the World

Lion's Gaze: A Commentary on the Tsig Sum Nedek

Mipham's Sword of Wisdom: The Nyingma Approach to Valid Cognition

The Nature of Mind (formerly titled *Pointing Out the Nature of Mind: Dzogchen Pith Instructions of Aro Yeshe Jungne*)

Prajnaparamita: The Six Perfections

Praise to the Lotus Born: A Verse Garland of Waves of Devotion

The Seven Nails: The Final Testament of the Great Dzogchen Master Shri Singha

The Smile of Sun and Moon: A Commentary on the Praise to the Twenty-One Taras

Supreme Wisdom: Commentary on Yeshe Lama (restricted)

Tara's Enlightened Activity

Uprooting Clinging: A Commentary on Mipham Rinpoche's Wheel of Analytic Meditation

OPENING THE DOOR OF THE DHARMA TREASURY PRACTICE GUIDES

A series of condensed instructions on some of the main practices of the Padmasambhava Buddhist Center and Nyingma lineage

More information about these and other works by the Venerable Khenpo Rinpoches can be found online at:

padmasambhava.org/chiso

Padmasambhava Buddhist Center

Venerable Khenchen Palden Sherab Rinpoche and Venerable Khenpo Tsewang Dongyal Rinpoche established the Padmasambhava Buddhist Center (PBC) to preserve the authentic message of Buddha Shakyamuni and Guru Padmasambhava in its entirety, and in particular to teach the tradition of Nyingmapa and Vajrayana Buddhism. It is dedicated to world peace and the supreme good fortune and well-being of all. PBC now includes over twenty centers in the United States, Russia, Canada, and Puerto Rico, in addition to monastic institutions in India, Russia, and the United States.

The Samye Translation Group was founded by the Venerable Khenpo Rinpoches to commemorate and preserve the great ancient tradition of translation that was firmly established during the glorious Tibetan Buddhist era of the seventh through tenth centuries. As a reflection of gratitude for the unique activities of these enlightened translators, the Samye Translation Group has published Dharma books that cover all nine yana teachings of the Nyingma school of Tibetan Buddhism, including shedra philosophy books.

For more information about the Venerable Khenpo Rinpoches' activities, the Samye Translation Group, or Padmasambhava Buddhist Center, please contact:

Padma Samye Ling
618 Buddha Highway
Sidney Center, NY 13839
(607) 865-8068
padmasmabhava.org

Padma Samye Chökhor Ling Monastery • Sarnath, India

Orgyen Samye Chökhor Ling Nunnery • Sarnath, India

Padma Samye Jetavan Miracle Stupa • Shravasti, India

Gochen Monastery • Tibet

Palm Beach Dharma Center • West Palm Beach, Florida

Palden Sherab Pema Ling • Jupiter, Florida

Yeshe Tsogyal Temple • Nashville, Tennessee

Padma Gochen Ling • Monterey, Tennessee

Pema Tsokye Dorje Ling • San Juan, Puerto Rico

Palden Padma Samye Ling • Sidney Center, New York

Dharma Protectors: Four-Armed Mahakala, Ekajati, Dorje Lekpa, and Rahula

ཨེ་གི་ནི་ཏུ་ཊ་ཊུག་པ་འདི་དབེ་ཚེའི་ནང་དུ་བཞགས་ན་དབེ་ཆ་དེ་ར་ཙ་འདུར་
བགོ་མས་ཀུང་ཉེས་པ་མེ་འབྱུང་བར་འརྨ་དཔལ་ཊ་རྒྱུད་ལས་གསུངས་སོ། །